3 DAYS
To A Pharmaceutical
Sales Job Interview!

WOW!

I've had some great success with your book! I've got something in the works with three major pharmaceutical companies who have open positions they are looking to fill in the short term. Having someone on the inside scoping things out really makes a difference. With your book, I've gotten some information that I would never have ordinarily been able to find on my own or on the web. Thank you!!!
— **Christine**

Dear Lisa,
I have followed the program and now have some very good leads. I live in Oklahoma City and am aggressively pursuing a career in pharmaceutical sales after a very successful career in the home improvement business. Since I have ordered your book, I have had several new contacts and am totally convinced that when I get into the industry it will be because of what I am doing by following your lead.
— **Kim Nicholson**

Lisa's book is exactly what I needed from the very beginning of my pharmaceutical sales job search. Had I had this book a month ago, I would have landed at least two of the jobs that I interviewed for. The questions that were asked in my interviews are exactly the questions that were listed in her book, and unfortunately I did not have the correct answers then, but I sure do now. I truly believe if I follow her step-by-step instructions, that landing another interview will not even be a question. I'm glad that I purchased it, it made all the difference in the world.
Sincerely,
— **Darci**

Great book for interview preparation!
I've been trying to break into medical sales for about three months and have secured an interview at a major pharmaceutical company. I did not buy or use this book to get interviews, but the section regarding the likely interview questions and the 'right' answers were very helpful. When you haven't worked in pharmaceuticals, it's hard to anticipate what a hiring manager is

going to ask and what they want your answers to be. I think I'm going into this interview much better prepared than I would have been otherwise, especially since she gives helpful hints on what a day in the life of a pharmaceutical rep is like. The book covers all of the bases in the how to interview department. It even included a section on how to sell the interviewer a "pen" which is usually required in these interviews. Also, a great section on situational interview questions and answers and a great comprehensive list of pharmaceutical companies and contact information. I highly recommend this excellent resource.
— **Kyle**

Lisa,
Thank you for your book! Since I have followed the program, I have made some terrific contacts. I have an interview this Monday with a company that does primarily generic drugs and acquires already existing brand labels. This is the first interview that I have had (after searching for several months) and am very excited. Thanks again!
— **Dan Dick**

Lisa,
I received your book in the mail yesterday, and I must say, I found it to be "very informative." I used the techniques that you said to use and "BANG" I had 13 different leads in 20 minutes!
Thank you for your advice!
— **Joseph W. Burris III**
    Future Pharmaceutical Sales Representative

Hi Lisa:
I received your program and it is very helpful — thank you! Before I sent for it I was not in the interview process. I am now scheduled to meet on Friday with a D.M. I completed the application paperwork and sent it to the D.M. so they could start checking me out. I really, really appreciate all of the insight that you and your book have given me — I'm almost there and I want to close the deal and get this job! Thanks!
— **Barbara Carlson**

Lisa,
I got a call tonight from the district manager offering me the job! He told me that he wanted to make me the offer last week but they had to process my background first. It's one of the Johnson & Johnson companies, great benefits and great people. I've met a total of six reps, three district managers and the regional manager. All of them have been very professional and seem like high caliber people — a very important factor in my decision. There IS a light

at the end of the tunnel — there IS a payoff to all of this hard work and preparation and I'm telling you — it feels GREAT to have people excited about you and what you can bring to their company! Thank you for your book and for personally answering all of my questions along the way. Reading *3 Days to a Pharmaceutical Sales Job Interview* has helped me tremendously during this "waiting game"!

— A very happy Steve

I wish you the best of luck with your hunt
for a pharmaceutical sales position!

I am always thrilled to get feedback about this program
so please inform me of your success stories.

email:
Lisa@PharmaceuticalSalesInterviews.com

— Lisa

Lisa Lane's

3 DAYS To A Pharmaceutical Sales Job Interview!

(Fourth Edition)

The "How To"
Book Of
Breaking Into
Pharmaceutical
Sales

www.PharmaceuticalSalesInterviews.com

Thank you for buying my book! I hope that you find it inspirational as well as full of good information.

Visit my website at *www.pharmaceuticalsalesinterviews.com* if you feel that you need any additional assistance or if you feel that you could benefit from any of my other pharmaceutical sales job search products listed below:

Targeted Resume Distribution:
I will personally email your resume directly to over 150 pharmaceutical, medical equipment, and biotech sales companies and recruiters. This service is a big time saver and is a very effective and inexpensive way to get your resume directly in front of the people who are looking to fill med/pharma field sales positions. This is a targeted service and will demand better results than if you were to post your resume on a job board or have it "blasted" to a job board. It will also give you access to companies who may not use the jobs boards to find candidates.

Interview Audio CD:
We have recruited the expertise of Lisa Alexander (**former Pfizer regional recruiter**) to help you master your interviews. Lisa's 65 minute audio CD demonstrates practice pharmaceutical sales interviews. Listen in and learn what to expect during interviews and how to effectively answer tough questions. This will surely help you to make the cut!

Resume tune up:
The resume tune up that we offer is for professionals who want a thorough analysis of their resume or want professional input to write their own resume. The resume tune up is a comprehensive, 30 minute, one-on-one phone meeting where your resume is analyzed for these 10 keys to landing pharmaceutical sales interviews:

Good luck, and good selling!

-Lisa

IF YOUR JOB
IS A PLEASURE,
LIFE IS A JOY!

When I was a pharmaceutical sales representative,
I truly enjoyed my job. I hope that this program
helps to bring joy to many.
— Lisa Lane

I ran across this quote while I was shopping in IKEA one day. I don't know who the author is. Funny thing was that it was printed on a sign near the home office furniture. I included this quote to motivate you so rip this page out and hang it on your refrigerator!

Lisa Lane's

3 DAYS
To A Pharmaceutical
Sales Job Interview!

(Fourth Edition)

TABLE OF CONTENTS

Pharmaceutical Sales Jobs:
The Requirements
and the Rewards

Careers in pharmaceutical sales have consistently ranked among the most rewarding careers in America. It's no wonder: base salaries range from $40,000–$60,000 and commissions/bonuses can add more than 50% to the base salary. Many companies also offer full benefits and a company car.

The rewards of employment in the pharmaceutical industry are easy to understand. High salaries, excellent benefits, and the knowledge that a drug you helped to distribute can improve or save lives are very appealing. Some of the extra perks include: full expense account, incentive prizes, and all expense paid trips to wonderful cities.

If you land one of these jobs, the career path is an excellent one. Once hired, you can expect to remain employed for a long time in an industry that puts its priorities on maintaining low turnover and rewarding excellent performance.

Many field representatives start their careers in sales and work their way up into specialty or hospital sales positions. There are also many opportunities in sales management and training, and product marketing, all of which are considered to be promotions from field positions. It is very common to see pharmaceutical representatives opt to remain in the field for a number of years. Most truly enjoy what they do for a living and are rewarded well for their efforts.

The minimum requirement for an entry-level position is usually a four-year college degree (to the surprise of many, any field will do). Sales experience is a plus but not a must and qualities most prized are leadership, an outgoing personality, and an entrepreneurial spirit and drive. If you also have documentable achievements, you can count those as feathers in your cap.

Recent college grads with the minimum requirements are encouraged to apply: they are often viewed as very motivated and easy to train. Generally, most companies allow their managers to make most of the hiring decisions. They usually hire proven leaders and achievers as well as people who can converse well and listen well, recent college grads included.

Food for thought:
In 2005, worldwide sales of prescription drugs is expected to be 588 billion dollars.

Landing Pharmaceutical Sales Jobs: Answers To Your Most Frequently Asked Questions

The following are my answers to some common questions about pharmaceutical sales. Please note that the answers here are open for interpretation and differing opinions. I offer my opinion and I believe that others in the industry would agree with these answers.

Q. Why are pharmaceutical sales jobs in such high demand?

A. Pharmaceutical sales careers have consistently ranked among the most rewarding careers in America. It is common knowledge that pharmaceutical companies treat their sales representatives exceptionally well. Most offer excellent salaries with commissions and outstanding benefits packages including company car. The extra perks include bonuses, incentive prizes, and all expense paid trips to wonderful cities. The fact that you don't have a boss to report to on a daily basis is an added perk!

Q. I have no sales experience/I am a recent college graduate. Do I still have a chance?

A. Yes, you do have a chance... a good chance! Pharmaceutical companies hire people with and without sales experience, including recent and new college grads. They hire people from all backgrounds including accountants, teachers, nurses, office managers, computer programmers, and marketing professionals to name just a few. Some companies and managers prefer sales experience but it is not a requirement. Generally, most companies allow their managers to make most of the hiring decisions. They usually hire the proven leaders and achievers as well as people who can converse well and listen well.

Q. How do I go about my job hunt?

A. The key to breaking into pharmaceutical sales is to work hard at getting in. Remember that you have a lot of competition. If you want to succeed, you have to work at getting noticed and you must cover all your bases.

First and foremost, start with an outstanding résumé. Consider professional assistance if this is not your area of expertise: I have seen a lot of résumés and minor changes can make a big difference. If you produce your own résumé, be sure to ask family, friends, and professionals in the business to critique it for you. Once your résumé is the best that it can be, get it out there. It's got a lot of work to do! Post it on job boards. Send it to recruiters. Bring it with you to career fairs. Reply to ads with it. Mail it out to the human resources departments of companies that interest you and don't forget that newspaper classified ads still exist. Tell everyone that you are pursuing a pharmaceutical sales position (you never know, a friend of a friend might have a great lead for you). And last but not least, follow this program. It will show you exactly what you need to do to secure interviews.

Q. I have posted my résumé on career websites and I have not gotten any interviews. Why?

A. Impactful, online résumés require you follow a separate set of rules from the traditional, printed résumé (refer to the e-résumés section of this book for advice). If you follow this program, you will have more success arranging interviews than if you were to simply post your résumé online.

In this industry, posting your résumé on jobsites is necessary but that alone is not enough. You can't assume that companies and recruiters will come to you: You must go to them.

Food for thought:

Approximately 40% of jobs that are posted online are either already filled or don't exist.

Q. I don't have a bachelor's degree. Will my business experience compensate for my lack of degree?

A. There are pharmaceutical reps with less schooling than a bachelor's degree but not many. In general, pharmaceutical companies can afford to be very selective simply because of the number of applicants per opening. Most companies have a four-year degree requirement. In some instances, managers will consider sales achievements in lieu of the degree. If you feel you have an exceptional résumé and decide to pursue this field with less than a four-year degree, keep in mind that your job search may take longer than the norm and you may have limited success.

Novartis is known to have hired reps with less than a four-year degree. When I worked for the company, a woman in my district had an associate's degree. While I can't say for sure how many of their reps fit into this category, my guess is that there are other companies that find exceptional people and are willing to hire them regardless of their formal education.

Rookie of the year!

Q. Am I too old to break into pharmaceutical sales?

A. No. Pharmaceutical companies hire from all age groups. Some of the top reps are experienced professionals. Keep in mind that most of the physicians you will be calling on are in their 40s and older. The philosophy of some companies and managers is that an older rep can relate on a more personal level with the physician and can also hold a more mature and meaningful conversation. There are many reps out there who are in their 20's but that is the exception rather than the rule.

Q. Do I need a science degree to break into pharmaceutical sales?

A. No. Pharmaceutical companies hire people with backgrounds that range from accounting to zoology. As a rule, all of the science that one needs to succeed in this industry is taught during the initial training period.

Q. Why will pharmaceutical companies hire English majors over Biology majors at times?

A. A science background is great but it doesn't guarantee that the person can sell. An English major with an exceptional GPA and an outstanding personality is a great potential hire. Chances are that she or he will excel in sales training and their personality will help them reach their sales goals.

Until very recently, there were no colleges that offered a "pharmaceutical sales" degree. Some universities have recently begun offering a bachelor of science degree in Pharmaceutical Science. One such school that I know of is the College of St. Catherine in St. Paul, Minnesota.

Q. What are the entry-level requirements for a pharmaceutical sales position?
A. Entry-Level Requirements:
- **Four-year bachelor's degree.** Some companies will consider sales experience in lieu of the degree. If you have a great résumé with documented sales success, you will have a shot at landing interviews.
- **GPA above a 3.0 preferred**
- **Driver's license with a good driving record** (a minor ticket or two won't hurt)

- **Pass credit and background checks** (if your credit rating is poor, you may have to use your own credit card for expenses and be reimbursed rather than have access to a company credit card.)

Preferred areas of study:
- **Chemistry**
- **Anatomy and Physiology**
- **Biology**
- **Marketing**
- **Communication**
- **Journalism**

Preferred professional degrees:
- **Pharmacy**
- **Nursing**
- **Medical Assistant**

Preferred experience:
- **Outside sales experience with documented success**
- **Previous pharmaceutical sales experience**

Note: You can still land a pharmaceutical sales job without possessing any of the "preferred" criteria.

Q. How important is my résumé?
A. Your résumé is a critical component of your job search: It is not uncommon for managers to receive more than 500 résumés for one advertised job opening. You have to give some time and attention to your résumé if you want to get attention in this sea of applicants (see the résumé tips in this program). If you are going to hire a professional to prepare your résumé, do your research before hiring one.

Q. How do I shop for a résumé writer?
A. Look for a résumé writer who specializes in sales or pharmaceutical sales and do the following:
1. Ask for referrals from satisfied customers.
2. Interview three or more companies and then make a decision based on the information that you gather.
3. Check with your local Better Business Bureau to make sure that there have been no complaints filed about the writer and/or the company.
4. Ask who actually prepares the résumé. Some companies "farm out" the work.

5. Ask if the writer/company offers a guarantee for the work. If you don't get any interviews with your résumé, will it be rewritten at no additional charge?

6. Ask about the cost and find out exactly what is included. Is a cover letter and a scannable version of the résumé provided?

Q. What type of benefits and perks do pharmaceutical companies offer their reps?

A. Pharmaceutical companies offer excellent benefits and perks to employees. This is especially true when it comes to what is offered to their sales reps. Their philosophy is a simple one: Reward your reps and they will stay motivated and happy. A motivated and happy rep = increased sales and motivated and happy reps in the sales force can equate to millions of dollars in profits. A good theory that works well!

Along with a substantial salary and commission plan, pharmaceutical reps can usually rely on company supplied health insurance, retirement plans, profit sharing, and tuition reimbursement. Reps can also expect to have a fully reimbursed expense account, including company car, as well as all expense paid trips to interesting locations for sales meetings and new product launches. Top performers can expect incentive prizes and vacations.

Q. I am a college student. What can I do NOW to increase my chances of securing a pharmaceutical sales job when I graduate?

JOB WINNING TIPS FOR COLLEGE STUDENTS:

To the surprise of many, pharmaceutical companies **do** hire recent college grads. (Merck happens to love hiring right out of college.) They look for extroverts who are motivated to succeed.

When you see an ad for an opening that requires two years prior sales experience, don't assume that you don't qualify for the job. They are listing the requirements for the perfect candidate but don't always hire the person with the sales experience. Many times, they will hire the recent college grad with the "potential" to excel in sales.

If you are still enrolled in college, do as much as you can now to better your chances of landing a pharmaceutical sales career when you graduate:

Take On Some Leadership Positions
    President of fraternity/sorority
    Resident assistant
    Fundraising chairperson
    Captain of rugby team
    Editor of school newspaper

Work On Your Communication Skills
  Take public speaking courses.
  Take interpersonal communication courses.
  Land a job as a tour guide for your school.

Show Your Selling Potential
  Take sales and marketing classes.
  Take on an outside sales job on a part-time basis.
  (Enterprise rent a car offers a well-respected training program for college students)

Learn The Ropes
  Work part-time in a pharmacy.
  Work in a doctor's office or HMO.

Show Your Compassionate Side
  Get involved in community service projects.
  Organize community events.
  Raise funds for a favorite cause.

It's Never Too Early To Network
  Land a preceptorship with a rep or two.
  (Ride with them to their calls for a day)

Strive For Great grades
  3.0 or better is preferred

Note: Completing any of the above will be a great addition to your résumé. Do as many as possible (without letting your GPA slip) and you will look like the recent college graduate with the "potential" managers are looking for.

How do pharmaceutical companies choose sales representatives?

This is a press release reprinted with permission by Medzilla.com
Pharmaceutical sales can be a tough area to break into—especially if you lack coveted sales experience. The fact is, if you have experience selling pharmaceuticals in a specific disease category or have contacts at major medical institutions, you might be a shoe in. However, for those who have limited sales experience or no sales background, the opportunities become more limited. Medzilla gets an insider's view about how pharmaceutical companies hire and what job candidates who want to launch careers as sales reps need to know.

FOR IMMEDIATE RELEASE

Marysville, WA (PRWEB) September 17, 2004 — If you are in the market for a job and have heard that pharmaceutical sales is a lucrative field, there are a few things you should know before completing that first online application or sending your résumé.

"Pharmaceutical sales is a tough, but not impossible, area to break into. What you need to know is that there are different categories of sales reps in the pharmaceutical arena, and each category tends to carry different requirements," says Frank Heasley, PhD, president and CEO of MedZilla.com, (*www.medzilla.com*) a leading Internet recruitment and professional community that serves biotechnology, pharmaceuticals, healthcare and science. "Even without prior pharmaceutical sales experience, you can get your feet in pharma company doors, but you have to know what hiring managers are looking for."

An inside perspective

John McCabe, senior director, Ventiv Recruitment Services, has a broad view of what major pharmaceutical companies look for when hiring their sales forces. Ventiv filled some 1,500 pharmaceutical sales positions last year and have filled about 1,000 such jobs so far this year.

According to McCabe, there are three general categories of reps in pharmaceutical sales: primary sales or mass-market representatives; specialty pharmaceutical sales reps; and hospital or institutional reps.

Entry level? Look for the primary sales position

Pharmaceutical sales positions, called primary care or mass-market representatives, typically include those entry-level positions where hiring managers are willing to look at recent graduates or people without a lot of previous sales experience.

These types of sales reps, according to McCabe, usually call on primary care physicians, such as family practitioners, promoting mass-market products. These products include first-line allergy, hypertension and other medications that these gatekeepers would commonly prescribe.

Experience needed: Specialty representatives

The next tier of pharmaceutical sales representative is the specialty representative, who specializes in a therapeutic area. One such representative might sell a women's pharmaceutical product geared for OB-Gyn prescribing, according to McCabe.

Usually, you are promoted from within the company to become a specialty sales representative. "So, generally the mass market or primary care sales representative is promoted into a specialty sales team," he says.

However, if a pharmaceutical employer is launching a new sales team, obviously it cannot promote their whole primary care sales team. In this scenario, the company might go outside the traditional thinking and look for others who are have related experience. If, for example, you have been selling a product that lowers cholesterol to the primary care market, a company looking for a specialty sales rep in cardiology might be interested in hiring you.

A general expectation among hiring managers who are looking for specialty pharmaceutical sales representatives is that job candidates bring a "brag book" to the interview, McCabe says. That book includes information about any products you've sold, sales reports that show you were a leader in your district or sales region, and more to depict your sales success.

A tier somewhere in between: Institutional or hospital reps
Institutional or hospital representatives call on university and other medical centers.

"They might sell the higher levels products that usually get sold to hospitals directly, like IV drugs, emergency medicine drugs, some of the HIV drugs," McCabe says. "We have specialists calling on oncologists in their offices, but if a specialist is selling radioactive materials for chemotherapy, then that person is usually calling on an institution or a hospital."

Employers look for sales experience in this category of sales representative—often specialty experience. If you've made calls on hospitals before, that will also look good on your résumé.

"Usually at the hospital level, [employers look for someone who knows decision-makers at those institutions," McCabe says.

Thinking like the employers think
Ventiv works with more than 36 pharmaceutical companies. According to McCabe, while each company has its own hiring profiles, generally speaking, they look for a blend of experience when hiring their sales forces.

"When we're helping build sales forces for those clients, the mix is usually something along the lines (and, again, this is generalized) of 30% to 40% of the sales force will have health care-related sales experience," he says.

By health-care related experience, McCabe means that you might have been selling pharmaceutical products, in the biotech arena, medical devices or consumer goods that are promoted in doctors' offices, such as over-the-counter antacids. In a broad sense, you would have experience selling to or calling on doctors, he says.

Another 30% to 40% of sales reps in a typical pharmaceutical company sales force are outside sales, or business-to-business sales candidates. Those are the people working for copier and other companies, which are not necessarily tied to health care.

"They have outside sales experience where they're calling on accounts; they have sales territories; they drive to their appointments; they're trying to build business for an organization; but they're not in pharmaceutical or health care sales," McCabe says. "The last tier, which is 10% to 30%, will have no sales experience. Those are recent college graduates; sometimes teachers; sometimes nurses and others with no sales experience.

"That's the typical distribution in most clients we see."

What are the odds?
For someone who has no or little sales experience coming into the industry, their only real chance is to get into those primary care-mass market areas, McCabe says. "For someone who has been in the industry and is looking for a step up, then they're usually qualified for the specialty or hospital sales type positions."

If you have no sales experience, there are certain standout traits that call the attention of hiring managers and recruiters, according to McCabe.

Your first step will be to get through the résumé screening. In that phase of hiring, employers and recruiters typically look at education and work history.

All pharmaceutical employers look for at least a four-year college degree for entry-level positions, McCabe says. The other important element is a consistent work history.

If you have a résumé with either work history gaps or multiple employers, make sure to explain those snafus in your cover letter or résumé, he says. "If there's a legitimate explanation, it's usually not an issue."

The next level of scrutiny is having some sales experience.

"Most companies have found that people who are successful selling other products can be successful selling pharmaceutical products," McCabe says.

The truth is that from 70% to 90% of the pharmaceutical sales force of any given company will have sales experience upon hiring, he says. "Then, [employers will take a chance on some recent grads who have a 4.0 GPA and maybe they worked their way through school or held offices at school or were leaders on sports teams. They'll usually take a chance on a small percentage … of people with a nursing background who know doctors in the area."

The bottom line

If you ask any manager what they're trying to hire, the answer is— they're trying to hire their next number one sales rep, McCabe says. "So, most of them will make the assumption that the only way that they're going to be the number one sales rep in a short period of time is if they know how to sell."

Still, according to Michele Groutage, Medzilla's director of marketing, there is hope for those with no sales experience but who know the roles. "We've seen people with no direct sales experience land jobs as pharmaceutical sales representatives," she says. "Nurses and others in health care have the benefit of their knowledge; teachers know how to educate. What those people have to do is highlight those aspects of their careers in which they've worked to 'sell' people on ideas or motivate people. They then have to come across with key sales characteristics in the interview."

About MedZilla.com

Established in mid 1994, MedZilla is the original web site to serve career and hiring needs for professionals and employers in biotechnology, pharmaceuticals, medicine, science and healthcare. MedZilla databases contain about 10,000 open positions, 13,000 résumés from candidates actively seeking new positions and 71,000 archived résumés.

Lisa Lane's

3 DAYS
To A Pharmaceutical
Sales Job Interview!

(Fourth Edition)

This program provides information for prospective pharmaceutical sales representatives. It outlines the most effective means of gaining sales employment with a pharmaceutical company.

The harder you work at this program the more successful you will be. If you are determined to be employed as a sales representative in the pharmaceutical industry, follow the program. Give it all you've got and you will reap the rewards.

The following section of this guidebook is a step-by-step guide which can lead to interviews with top pharmaceutical companies. The hours suggested are intended as a guideline and many people find that less time is needed than is outlined in the program. Follow along. You be the judge of how much time is required.

CARPE DIEM!
(Seize the day)

This program requires you to take **action!**

You are the master of your own destiny.

Pharmaceutical sales managers look to hire creative, hardworking, extroverts. Your goal when following this program is to be the diamond on this grid.

Creative
Innovative
Motivated

Lackadaisical   Hardworking
                                                 Enthusiastic
                                                 Go-Getter
                                                 Friendly

Unimaginative

WHEN YOU FOLLOW THIS PROGRAM,
YOU WILL FIND THAT
ACTION = INTERVIEWS!

Section 1:
3 Days to a Pharmaceutical Sales Job Interview!

▷ ▷ ▷

CONGRATULATIONS!
YOU ARE ON YOUR WAY TO GETTING INTERVIEWS!

You are about to follow a program which will show you how to locate pharmaceutical sales job openings, how to make contacts with the right people, and how to impress those responsible for hiring. Before you begin, remember that you never get a second chance to make a first impression. Take some time before you begin the program to make sure you are prepared to make a great first impression.

Consider this checklist before you get started:

1. Is your résumé the best that it can be? Have you proofread it and gotten critiques from family and friends? Can you honestly look at it and say that you would interview yourself if you were doing the hiring? Your résumé must be as presentable as you are. It's a reflection of you. If you want to land a job as a pharmaceutical representative, you have a lot of competition. Your résumé must be the best of the best. No wrinkles, no typos, please (refer to the résumé section of this book for some help)!

Make your résumé one that you are proud of and make at least 50 copies of it for this program [*Note:* Professional résumé writers recommend 24 lb. white, at least 88 lumens and always printed on a laser printer (not inkjet)].

Résumé Reviewer: **Suggested Changes:**

2. Do you have a professional appearance? Pharmaceutical managers like their reps to be immaculate, well-dressed, and clean cut. Make sure your hair has a new trim and that your nails are well-manicured. You will also need a nice business casual outfit for this program. If you don't have one, invest in one and don't skimp on the shoes: You've got to look great from head to toe. You will be going out and meeting pharmaceutical reps and pharmacists you will want to impress while you follow this program.

3. Are you motivated and excited? Let your enthusiasm show: Enthusiasm is contagious. If your enthusiasm for getting a job shows while you are making your contacts, people you meet will be more apt to help you in your search.

 A word from Lisa:

If you are serious about starting a career as a pharmaceutical sales representative, be assured that this program will put you on the right track to gaining employment with a pharmaceutical company.

My goal in offering this program is to help you land interviews and shorten your job hunt. I cannot go arrange interviews for you. That part of the program is up to you. You will ultimately determine how many interviews you get.

It is very important to dedicate yourself to your goal of getting interviews. Commit yourself to completing the program as it was designed. Don't sell yourself short. Complete dedication is required to ensure the success of this program. A little time invested now will have a big payoff down the road.

This program is designed to be followed on three consecutive days. You will need to complete Day 1 of the program during a weekday because you will be making contacts with pharmaceutical reps who work Monday through Friday. The best advice I can offer is to start the program when you know you can complete it in the timeframe outlined. If you leave gaps between the steps, you will not be as successful. Put your mind to it, put your sales personality to work, get going, and good luck!

One pharmaceutical sales employment ad in the *New York Times* often attracts more than 500 résumés. Why compete with those numbers? This program will show you how to land interviews before the job openings are advertised. You have much better odds of landing the job when you are one of only a few being considered for the position.

Food for thought:

There are currently more than 90,000 pharmaceutical sales reps in the U.S. and most of these positions are filled by personal referral.

75% of all pharmaceutical sales job openings are never advertised!

DAY 1: LOCATING UNADVERTISED JOB OPENINGS

This is a very important day! There are many open territories right there in your own backyard. Your job today is to locate them all. Simply follow the program and you will be amazed at how many opportunities there are for the asking. The harder you work at this step the more successful you will be at finding those openings and landing interviews.

The first thing that you need to recognize is the potential for openings. In any given area, there could be upwards of a hundred pharmaceutical companies with several sales forces selling their products. Many larger companies have diverse product lines and have several divisions with representatives who call on various specialists. Some companies have different division names and could potentially have several reps calling on the same physicians for various products. Keep that in mind today as you go about your business. There are always openings due to company expansions, promotions, maternity, reps changing companies, and, believe it or not, people leaving the industry.

Example of Company Sales Force Divisions

These divisions were fabricated for the sake of the example and do not reflect the current sales divisions at these companies. Companies are constantly reorganizing their sales forces and it would be impossible to keep an up-to-date list.

Company:	Division:	Status:
Schering Plough	Respiratory	Filled
	Allergy/Immunology	**Open**
	Key (Flextime)	Filled
Glaxo-Smith Kline	Cardiovascular	Filled
	Respiratory	**Open**
	Hospital	Filled
	Oncology	**Opening next month**
Pfizer	Pediatric	Filled
	Ob-Gyn	Filled

Get excited! Most of the open positions that you will locate will be unadvertised. You are on the inside track! When you are on the inside track, you have an excellent chance of securing interviews. You may be one of only a few people who know about this position. Most managers will interview candidates referred by their reps before they publicize the opening.

Locating the openings:

Get started by locating the largest medical office building in your area. Find this by looking in the phone book under "physicians." Look for the address where most of the physicians are practicing. Be sure that they all have different phone numbers: You don't want to find one large group office. Locate a medical building with various specialists practicing independently or in small groups in one building. You also want to avoid locating an HMO building or a hospital. If there are no large medical buildings listed, locate a large medical office park. This is where most pharmaceutical sales representatives conduct their business.

Once you have located the building, prepare to go there. Dress in your best business casual clothing (no jeans, no suits). Pick a nice day and pack a lunch. Grab a pen, a pad, and all 50 copies of your well-prepared résumé. Bring several copies of the lead organizer located at the back of this program and drive to the medical building. Prepare to arrive before 9 a.m. and prepare to stay a while. The longer you stay, the more contacts you will make.

Park in a space near the main entrance and be on the lookout for pharmaceutical reps. They are easy to find because they fit a mold: They're dressed in suits, are often found rummaging around their trunks and carry rather large sample bags. Many wear nametags. They'll be swarming the building in no time and will be in and out of the building all day long. It's not unusual for one busy practice to have 5–10 reps calling on them in one day. If you have selected a busy office building, you should see a lot of reps. If you can't get a parking space with a good view of the main entrance, go inside the building and make yourself comfortable in the lobby.

When you spot a rep, allow them to do their business and prepare to say hello to them on their way out.

Meeting pharmaceutical reps:

Introduce yourself and get right to the point. Tell them that you are looking to land a career in pharmaceutical sales. Have no fear. Chances are good that they will go out of their way to help you out: after all, they were in your shoes at one time or another! Ask if they know of any openings in their district or any other divisions in the area. Ask for their card and make note of any openings on it. If they do know of an opening, get some details and ask if you can call them this evening at home for additional information. If their home number is not on their card, be sure to ask for it.

Before leaving, ask them if they know of any other employees from other companies who may know of additional openings. Many reps collect other rep cards. They may even have a personal stash of business cards in their car. Collect as many rep names and numbers as possible from each person you meet.

After gathering as much information as you can from him/her, thank them for their time and shake their hand firmly. Hand them a copy of your résumé and tell them you'll call tonight (if you can't call tonight, do this step on another day. You want to be fresh on their minds and appear to be very motivated). Quickly transfer this information onto the Lead Organizer (provided at the back of this program). You will want to keep all of this information neat and organized. You will be meeting a lot of people today: Don't allow your information to get mixed up. Numbers and contacts can all start to look alike after a while if you are not organized.

Repeat this step all day long (or for as long as you can). Continue to introduce yourself to reps and **DON'T** leave for lunch. Many reps get their best appointments at lunchtime. You'll want to be there to say "hello." You may encounter a rep who has catered a lunch for a doctor's office. Consider offering to help them carry it in and introduce yourself. Catch up with them again on their way out.

Don't hesitate one bit on this step!

The more reps you meet face-to-face, the more successful you will be at locating openings. They will also be more apt to help you with your job search if they have met you, know what you look like, and are familiar with your personality. Be confident, friendly and straightforward. Relax and let your personality shine. Pharmaceutical reps are "people people." They enjoy meeting other people and love to talk about what they do. They also work alone so they're happy to have someone to talk to. Most of them will be happy to help you out. If you are lucky, you may even run into a gathering of reps at a trunk (sounds funny, but it's something that reps do). They don't have offices to socialize in and a trunk is the next best place to mingle with others in the industry.

Many reps also get a cash reward if they refer someone who eventually is hired, so helping you is in their best interest. If you feel so inclined, you may also ask the rep for a preceptorship (where you ride with them for a day or a part of the day in their territory). This is a great chance to get to know them and the job. It's also a great addition to your résumé.

Creative idea for Day 1:

The following was sent to me via email by one of my customers and reprinted with her permission. Here is her message to me, verbatim:

Hi Lisa,

It was a very full, and fun, day "in the field" (i.e. parking lots and building lobbies) meeting pharmaceutical reps. I did receive 2 job opening leads which I have already followed up on. I gave my résumé to 14 different Reps (from different companies). I am planning on going back to "the field" for at least two more days, including making some visits to hospital pharmacies to ask about rep contacts there. As you suggested, the reps I met were (mostly) very friendly and interested in listening and helping.

The strategy I used was to have professional folders already prepared with a cover letter and two copies of my résumé enclosed — along with a professional business card I developed for myself that identifies me as a "Future Pharmaceutical Sales Representative" with my contact information on it (phone, email, address). That little twist was a great icebreaker and garnered several smiles and raised eyebrows!

Thank you again for your encouragement and assistance. I will let you know when I land that job!

Kind Regards,

Dianne
Tucson, Arizona

(Below is Dianne's business card; see page 34 for Dianne's cover letter)

Telephone:	E-Mail:
123-456-7890	futurerep@aol.com

Dianne
Future Pharmaceutical Sales Representative

123 Main Street, Anytown, USA 12345

Dianne's cover letter:

(Included in the presentation folder along with her résumé and business card)

Date: October 2, 2004

To: Pharmaceutical Sales Representatives, Tucson territory

Thank you for the opportunity to introduce myself. When I began researching my career change, I knew pharmaceutical sales was for me! I have what it takes to be your successful colleague and last week I was offered a sales representative position with a major pharmaceutical company. Unfortunately, the offer was for a position in Salt Lake City and I just relocated to Tucson four months ago. So my search continues for a territory opening in southern Arizona, preferably one that includes the Tucson market.

My professional background includes nine years as a self-employed, very successful business owner in Michigan and 15 years in healthcare — as an RN, with a four year degree from University of Michigan, and a dynamic, progressive hospital administration career. I've taught nursing pharmacology, have been a member of hospital Pharmacy & Therapeutic committees, and I know my way around hospitals, pharmacies, and physician practices. I have the professional qualities, skills, and enthusiastic drive to achieve results in pharmaceutical sales.

For the past year, I have been preparing for my career transition to pharmaceutical sales. My initiative has included extensive research of the industry and of pharmaceutical companies and their products. I have been networking with sales reps, including completing a field preceptorship with a Johnson & Johnson Senior Sales Specialist in Tucson. I have an unending intellectual curiosity, the ability to convey complex information, tireless energy, strong sales skills, and accountability to know my products, customers, competition, and business environment. I enjoy working as a team and I have proven ability to work independently to achieve significant results.

I am eager for the opportunity to apply my energy, sales skills, depth of healthcare knowledge and experience, and well developed business acumen to the challenges and rewards of pharmaceutical sales. No one will work harder to deliver more value and produce more results for your company.

My home office is prepared and I am available to begin employment immediately. I am enclosing my résumé for your consideration and would welcome a phone call or email if you become aware of an opening or anticipated opening with your company in the Tucson territory. I know that many Pharmaceutical Sales Representative positions are "inside track" opportunities and I sincerely appreciate any tips you can provide in this very competitive job market.

Thank you again for your time and consideration. I hope that our paths cross again in the near future and I look forward to being your road warrior colleague!

Most Sincerely,

Dianne

Helpful Tip:
Put an anecdotal comment on the back of the business cards that you gather, something that was unique or memorable about the rep or your conversation. This will help you to remember the rep and not confuse them with others whom you have met. This is called an "anchor".

This aspect of the program may initially seem awkward. After all, the thought of approaching a complete stranger and asking them for help in finding a job is not something that we do every day. Keep in mind, pharmaceutical reps are generally a friendly, helpful bunch of people. Simply approach one and you will see exactly what I am talking about. Sparking up a conversation with this group of people is as easy as talking to an old friend.

Customer Feedback: Proof that this method works!

Lisa,

   After leaving the military to pursue a career in pharm sales, I followed your program exactly and met over 20 reps in two days. All of them were open and receptive to me....just like you said they would be! I actually met a district manager who was doing a "ride along" with one of his reps on my first day! Within a week, he called me for an interview. A week later, I went to a second interview then rode for a day in the field with one of his "star" reps. The next day I met with the district manager and the regional manager and....they offered me the job!!!!! I am SO excited about this opportunity!! I am living proof that by following your program someone with no sales experience can truly "break in" to pharmaceutical sales!

Thank you so much for your help,

David

After you've met several reps, take an hour or so out of the day to find additional openings. Go door-to-door to the doctors' offices in the building but don't go at lunchtime (from 11 a.m.–1 p.m.). Introduce yourself to the receptionist and tell him/her that you're looking for a pharmaceutical sales position and that you would appreciate any leads they could supply you with. In particular, you would like to get some reps names and numbers. Most offices keep a file of reps cards and if you're lucky you might even be rewarded with the entire file. Be prepared to write down a lot of names and phone numbers.

If the office looks busy, come back later. Many offices close at 4 p.m. so be prepared to get all the information by then.

Not all receptionists will be friendly. Don't let a not-so-friendly receptionist or a "Nurse Ratchet" (as we used to call them) put a halt to your networking efforts. If one doesn't help you, chances are good that there's one in the building who will be helpful. Don't stop until you find him/her.

Going door-to-door is a necessary step because it allows you to locate potential openings for various divisions within a company. For example, Glaxo may have one rep that calls on internists and another specialty rep from their Allen and Hanbury's division that calls on pulmonologists. A rep from Glaxo may not know of openings in divisions other than his or her own.

Your goal today is to locate as many openings as possible. Don't sell yourself short. Use your sales personality to find them.

Contacts:

Company Name:	Division:	Contact Name/ #:	Opening? Y/N

DAY 1 (EVENING): CALL ALL OF THOSE LEADS!

Once you've gathered as much information as possible at the medical building, go home and sort through your organized information. Hopefully you've gotten a handful of cards, a long list of names and numbers and, most importantly, several leads on openings.

Use the table on page 37 to make a comprehensive pharmaceutical company contact list (you may need to make another copy or two). As you meet reps, you will become aware of the various divisions within each company. Keep track here and try to contact all reps from all divisions. Use the pharmaceutical company listing at the back of this book as a reference.

6–8:30 P.M.:

This is an exciting step! It's time to call all those friendly pharmaceutical reps you met who have leads for you. Before you start your calls, prepare to ask the right questions. You will want to spend time with each of them and make the most of their valuable information.

The phone call: What to say.

First and foremost, don't assume that they remember you from your meeting earlier today. They've been busy interacting with receptionists, physicians, nurses, office staff, and other reps all day. Take the first moments of the conversation to reintroduce yourself and thank them for taking the time to talk with you. Reiterate your enthusiasm for getting into the field of pharmaceutical sales.

Find out more about the opening:

Use the organizer sheets at the back of the program to take notes.

Mention the opening that they referred to and ask these important questions:
• What division has the opening?
• What specialists do they call on?
• What products will you be selling?

- Where is the territory?
- What are some competing products?
- Why is the position open?

The more that you find out about the position the better. This information will help you prepare for your interview.

Once you've broken the ice and gotten information about the position, ask about the district manager (DM).

Be sure to ask all of these very important questions about the district manager: The district manager is usually the person who conducts the initial interviews and eventually makes the final decision as to who is hired. The more you know about him/her, the better your chances of nailing the interview.
- Who had the position prior to its opening?
- What is the manager looking for in a rep?
- What would their ideal candidate be like?
- Likes/dislikes in a candidate?
- Managers hobbies/interests?

Tell the rep you will be sending a résumé to the manager and ask if you can mention the rep's name in a cover letter. Ask for the manager's e-mail address and his/her home address.

Note: Some managers don't like their reps to give out their home addresses. Use some finesse if the rep is hesitant to provide the information. Assure the rep that you are only asking for the information as a site to mail your résumé. Explain to the rep that you don't want to be one of the masses sending your résumé to a post office box. Ask them if they can help you out (they all know their managers' home address. It's where their weekly paperwork is sent).

If the rep will not provide the manager's home address, ask if you can have the manager's voicemail number or email address. When you call, leave a message telling the manager that you have met with their rep and would like to send a résumé to their home address for consideration. The manager may be willing to call you back with it or email it to you. Worst case scenario, you can email your résumé directly to him or her.

If you feel that you have developed a good rapport with the rep, ask if he/she would be willing to send the manager a copy of your résumé with a referral. If the rep is willing to do this for you, be sure to mail the rep another copy of your résumé with a stamped envelope. If the rep prefers, send a copy via email so that it can be forwarded on with his recommendation. Be sure to include a thank you for the referral. See the templates at the back of the program for suggestions.

After you have gathered all this information, thank the rep for his/her valuable time and get the rep's address if it was not on the card. Before hanging up ask, once again, if he/she might have additional leads for you (they may have access to many more rep cards in a file at home).

Repeat this step with the reps you met earlier today until 8:30 p.m. and save the remainder for tomorrow evening.

Notes: _____

_____

_____

_____

_____

_____

_____

_____

_____

_____

_____

_____

_____

_____

_____

_____

_____

_____

_____

Pharmacy Call Sheet:

■ Pharmacy Name: _____

Pharmacist: _____

Company Name/Division	Rep. Name	Rep. Number

DAY 2 (MORNING): HEAD OUT TO SOME PHARMACIES!

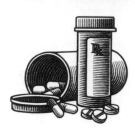

9 a.m. to noon:

Once again, you are on the hunt for job openings. Today you will be finding your leads from yet another valuable resource: your local pharmacists. It's important to know that pharmaceutical reps don't actually sell to pharmacists but many reps do check in on them for information on product movement, special pharmacy promotions, and doctor information.

Some reps spend more time in pharmacies than others do; and nonetheless, many pharmacists have insight on openings from reps who have been in. If the pharmacist doesn't know of any openings, chances are good that he or she may have a file full of rep names and numbers who do.

Ask the pharmacist if he or she knows of any openings and if they might be able to share some reps names and numbers with you. Most pharmacists are friendly people, particularly if you catch them when they aren't busy. Your best bet is to call on them either mid-morning or mid-afternoon. Try to avoid lunch and rush hour during weekdays — those tend to be busy times.

Note: Pharmacists are generally easy to talk to but not all of them keep good rep records. You may find that they have rep cards who are no longer in the area. Go to several large pharmacies to guarantee yourself good coverage. Try going to both large and small pharmacies. Sometimes the local "ma and pa" store is not as busy and can be a good place to gather information and get a good chat in with the pharmacist. Make a few copies of the Pharmacy Call Sheet to keep track of your leads and contacts.

Sample Personalized Referral Page:

Insert Manager's Name

Enclosed please find:

Insert your name résumé and cover letter.

Applying for the sales representative position
in the _____ territory.

Referred by: **Insert referring rep's name**

*Managers always give preference to candidates
who have been referred by their reps.
This additional page reminds them
every time they thumb through résumés.*

Meeting face to face with pharmacists is a great networking plan!

Hey Lisa,

Just wanted to take a minute to check in with you and say "Hi". A little over 2 years ago, I got a job as a pharmaceutical rep. I just recently got promoted to CNS specialty rep calling on neurologists. I really enjoy what I do and couldn't be happier.

Thanks so much for your help and your program. I actually got hired as a result of going into a pharmacy and collecting pharmaceutical rep cards and calling them. One just happened to pay off.

Thanks,

Kim N.

DAY 2 (AFTERNOON):
TAILOR YOUR RÉSUMÉ AND COVERS LETTERS TO MEET THE NEEDS OF THE DISTRICT MANAGERS

The personal touch goes a long, long way!

By now, you've gotten excellent leads and a lot of very useful information to help you land interviews. You're on the inside track! Now it's time to show your creative side (a trait that managers like) and let the interviews roll in.

Spend the afternoon today preparing your résumé and cover letters for mailing. You will be mailing them out to the managers with openings in their district.

Every salesperson knows that successful salespeople identify the needs of their customers and then show the customer how their product meets their needs. Today, you are the product. You already know what the managers are looking for from talking with their reps. Show them that you are just the person they are looking to hire!

Refer back to your notes and custom-design both your résumé and cover letter to meet the needs of each manager. Yes, this is a time consuming task but the effort is worth every minute spent. For example: You find out that a particular manager is looking for a sales rep with a creative rather than aggressive sales personality. Be sure to show him/her in the objective of your résumé as well as in the first paragraph of your cover letter that you are the creative person the manager is looking for. Be sure to back up the claim with examples.

The key to getting noticed is to find a connection with the person who will be doing the interviewing! Managers generally interview only a handful of applicants for each opening and they tend to hire people they like and can get along with. They will often hire someone that they like over someone with more experience.

Prepare a separate, personalized referral page to include on top of your cover letter. Center this information on the sheet. Keep it simple and to the point. (See page 38.)

Stuff your envelopes but don't address them: Put the name of the person who referred you on the outside of your envelope. Make the name rather large and bold but don't mail them yet. Put them aside until tomorrow (you will be putting the envelope inside another package; details to follow).

DAY 2 (EVENING): CALL YOUR OTHER LEADS

6 p.m.-8:30p.m.:
After you've called all of the reps you've met, prepare to call the people you were referred to who you haven't met. Unfortunately, you don't have the advantage of having met these people but have no fear.

Prepare to make calls.

- Introduce yourself and tell them where you got their name.

- Tell them that you're looking for leads on pharmaceutical sales openings in the area.

- Tell them how hard you're working at this and that you've spent a day at a medical office building. Once they've heard your story, they'll be bound to feel your enthusiasm and help you out.

- Ask if they are aware of any openings in their company and if they know of any other reps who may know of any.

If you find that they know of an opening in their district, jump back to the questioning about the details of the position and the manager.

Continue this step until 8:30 p.m.

DAY 3 (MORNING):
KNOCK THEIR SOCKS OFF!

Here's your chance to shine! If you follow this step, you'll be the creative person those managers have been looking for. They'll be so impressed that they will want to meet you. **Don't skip this crucial next step!**

Your goal at this point is to knock their socks off, get the attention you deserve, and lock in an interview! Managers are looking to hire creative sales reps. They are looking for people who can differentiate themselves from the crowd of reps who are calling on doctors. Knowing this, you need to personalize your mailing to show your creative side.

Go back to your notes and prepare to go *shopping* (yes, even if you are a male and hate to shop, get out to the mall).

You have a lot of important information about each manager including insight into his or her hobbies and interests. Use this information to your advantage and buy the manager a small something that proves to him or her that you've done your homework. Buy something useful but not expensive: You don't want to give the impression that you're buying an interview.

For example; if you find that several managers are golfers, you may want to buy packages of golf tees. Wrap several of them up with a small note that says "I fit your district to a tee" or "I'm a tee-rific salesperson." Write something that fits your personality. These examples might not be appropriate for your personality type. The point is to mail your résumé so that it gets noticed. If you can't come up with any creative ideas that suit the managers' hobbies, try some of these more generic gift ideas that all managers will appreciate:

1. Buy a small desk calendar and send it along with a note that says; Don't go another day without interviewing **insert your name** for the **insert territory location** territory.

2. Buy a box of pencils and send it along with a note that says; Call **insert your name** for the **insert territory location** territory. She/he is the sharpest one for the job!

3. Buy a To-Do list and send it along with a note that says; To do: Call **insert your name** at **insert your phone** number for the opening in the **insert territory location** territory.

Package your creative gifts and mail them to the **home addresses** of the managers. **Be sure to include your résumé, cover letter, and the cover sheet with the referring rep information.** Be sure to package them so they are neat and professional.

We all know that everyone opens his or her packages. This technique is a sure way to be noticed and to get your résumé read — it won't be added to a pile somewhere to be opened later.

Don't forget to send thank you notes to the people who referred you. You'll want to stay fresh in their minds and get good recommendations from them. Refer to the template section at the back of the program for ideas.

Food for thought:

Put yourself in the managers' shoes. Which would you open?
1. A run-of-the-mill résumé mixed in with hundreds of others in your P.O. box?
2. A package that came to your home address?

If you were the manager, whom would you interview?
1. One of the hundreds of applicants who responded to your ad on Monster.com?
2. The creative candidate who sent you the package and has been recommended by one of your reps?

Additional networking suggestions:

Take advantage of your Alma Mater. Their career services director can let you know if any pharmaceutical companies are recruiting on campus. They may also have contact information for alumni who are currently employed in the pharmaceutical industry.

Hotels (Yes, hotels!) are a great place to network for pharma sales jobs. Call their sales and catering department and ask which pharma companies will be having meetings in the coming weeks. If you call the big chains like Marriott and Hilton, you may be amazed at how many pharma companies plan to make use of their facilities for meetings. (A real jackpot would be a manager's meeting. Grab their attention at a break and work an entire room of people who do the hiring and don't forget your résumé!)

Notes: _____

_____

_____

_____

_____

_____

_____

_____

_____

_____

_____

_____

_____

_____

_____

_____

DAY 3 (AFTERNOON INTO EVENING): FINISH UP YOUR UNFINISHED BUSINESS.

Spend the remainder of this day preparing your résumé and cover letters for any additional leads. Spend this evening calling any additional people you need to follow up with.

Last but not least:

Put a professional greeting on your answering machine and prepare to screen your calls. In a day or two, those managers will be getting the packages that you sent and will be eager to talk with you. Your phone is about to start ringing!

Your first interview is typically a phone interview. Managers use the phone to get a feel for the personality of applicants and because you won't get a second chance to make a first impression, you should screen your calls. You won't get the opportunity to interview face-to-face if you don't do well on the phone; don't get caught off guard. Let the manager leave a message, then do your homework. Research the company and the products. Brush up on the name of the person who referred you and review the details of the position and the manager. Prepare to ask intelligent questions and give intelligent answers and then return the call within 24 hours.

Check out Hoovers and Bloomberg online for company background and financial data. Refer to RxList online for prescribing information or look it up in the *Physicians Desk Reference* at your local library (refer to the reference page at the back of this program).

CONGRATULATIONS!
This completes the *3 Days to a Pharmaceutical Sales Job Interview* section of this guidebook. Use the remaining information to help make your job hunt as successful as possible.

As they say in the pharmaceutical sales business world:

Stay focused and stay motivated.
Good luck and good selling!

Section 2:
Rev Up
Your
Résumé!

▷ ▷ ▷

REV-UP YOUR RÉSUMÉ!

Over the years, I have seen thousands of résumés. Of the résumés submitted, approximately 70% are good, another 25% are bad, and approximately 5% are outstanding. Bottom line: If you want to break into this competitive industry, you must have a top-notch résumé. You need a résumé that stands out.

A great résumé catches the attention of the person who is reviewing the résumé and doesn't necessarily mean that you have the best experience and qualifications. Carefully crafted words and layout techniques can make the difference between a résumé that is good and one that results in an interview.

How can you "kick it up a notch" and get your résumé out of the ranks of good and into the ranks of greatness? The next few pages are dedicated to helping you do just that. The first thing you need to do is to be aware of these common pharmaceutical sales résumé pitfalls. Avoid having your résumé fall into the same pit, so to speak.

> **Pharmaceutical Sales Résumé Pitfalls:**
> **Tips for staying out of the pit**
>
> As a general rule, most pharmaceutical sales résumés
> that are submitted fall short in these areas:
> 1. Length
> 2. Not a sales oriented résumé

1. Length:

The majority of pharmaceutical sales résumés that are submitted are too long. Time and again, the one page résumé has proven to be the most effective for landing pharmaceutical sales interviews. Put the best that you have to offer on one page and capture the readers' attention!

If you have a long list of achievements that you want to include on your résumé, find a way to get it all onto one page. A quality one-page résumé that beams with highlighted achievements will land interviews. If you save a long list of awards for a second page, you should assume it will not be read. On average, managers receive more than 500 résumés per advertised job opening. You can bet that they are not reading more than one page on the initial screening and if your résumé doesn't make the cut at first glance, it will rarely be looked at again.

How do your shorten your résumé?

Look at your job descriptions. Use the very effective bullet format (see samples) and give a brief description of your duties. As a rule, keep only those job duties that most mirror the responsibilities of a pharmaceutical rep. Keep the sales keywords and avoid using too many action verbs.

Just for fun!

Job description no-no:

Here is an actual job description from a résumé that was mailed to me. If I showed you the actual three page résumé, you would be bored so I have spared you the details.

Can you write a shorter, more effective version of these job duties?

Personally, I have a hard time condensing it. It's so wordy that I have a difficult time figuring out what this person actually did at this job!

Counselor/Technician: May 1996–Present:
• Combined patient care and clinical expertise with understanding of pharmacological therapy practices critical to patient well being. Lead successful recovery for two dual diagnosis psychiatric treatment facilities. Established guidelines and priorities. Identified real resources, effective channels and proven processes to improve and ensure long-term positioning. Developed knowledge in areas of psycho-pharmacotherapy. Created, updated and implemented company-wide patient care programs; assessed, reassessed, planned, and evaluated. Provided assistance for psychotherapeutic interventions, communicated with patients, lead group sessions, attended patient conferences, family conferences, and interaction; lead unit goal orientation and focus groups; charted patient progress.

• Lead educational efforts providing information on medications and pharmacotherapy compliance; Assisted in monitoring effects and provided documentation of various antipsychotics, mood stabilizing antidepressants, anticonvulsants, antianxiety agents, sedative agents, and c.n.s. stimulants.

- Authored and presented documentation on client progress and treatment plans; provided diagnosis education to clients/client members through oral communications and family conferences; included understanding of unit goal and treatment information.

- Orchestrated wide variety of activities on a daily basis, including staff collaborations; developed and implemented therapeutic goals while overseeing patient stabilization programs, ICU services and unit interventions.

- Honored multiple times with Eagle Award for outstanding professionalism for working above and beyond the call of duty while providing exceptional clinical service to patients.

The end!
WOW!

If you want interviews, write a concise, one-page résumé that is eye-catching and full of achievements. Boldface your best achievements.

2. Not a sales oriented résumé:

Many résumés are not written for a sales position. Put yourself in the manager's shoes. Think of the skills they are looking for and include them in your résumé.

Skills that managers are looking for:

- Excellent communicators.
- Public speakers.
- Good listeners.
- Closers.
- Capable of interacting with all levels of management.
- Capable of relaying scientific information.
- Capable of communicating with physicians from ivory tower areas (areas where docs are difficult to see and tend to have big egos).
- Creative. (If you want to ever sell to the docs in the ivory tower areas, you'll need creative ways of gaining access to them.)
- Outstanding work ethic.
- Organized.
- Ability to prioritize tasks.
- Ability to interpret sales data.

- Capable of getting reports in on time. Late paperwork is a pet peeve of many managers, if your work is late, so is theirs.
- Leadership abilities.
- Active participant at meetings.
- Capable of reading and memorizing scientific information.
- Self motivated.
- Works well on own without direct supervision.
- Entrepreneurial skills.

When describing your duties, use sales-related keywords and incorporate percentages and numbers to add to your credibility. If you've had sales experience, you have to show what you are capable of. For keyword ideas, see the e-résumés section.

If you've had a job that was not a sales position, but had duties and requirements that would apply to a sales job, mention them. If possible, tweak your job title to better match what a sales manager would be looking for.

Example:
The position of personal trainer could easily be called fitness sales/instruction. The job description should emphasize recruitment of clients and the management and communication skills involved rather than your knowledge of muscle groups and equipment.

TYPES OF RÉSUMÉS:

Chronological: Most employers prefer this type of résumé; It is particularly effective for sales résumés. The emphasis is on employment with the most recent job listed first. If your strengths lie in your work history and skills, this type of résumé is an excellent choice.

Functional: Employment is summarized or left off. Skills and achievements are highlighted. This format allows you to highlight education and talents. The functional résumé is often a good format for a recent college graduate with little or no work experience.

Combination: Combines the functional and chronological formats. Skills and accomplishments are listed first followed by employment history.

16 SURE SHOT WAYS TO FIRE UP YOUR RÉSUMÉ:

1. Keep your résumé to one page. Fill it with the best that you have to offer.
2. Include an objective that specifically states you are in search of a pharmaceutical sales position (sample objectives are listed at the bottom of this section).
3. List the company that you are applying to in the objective. It adds a personal touch and eliminates the mass produced look.
4. Be sure to include your home email address. Because email is an effective and efficient way to communicate with job applicants, managers use it often.
5. **Bold** your awards, leadership positions, and special achievements. By highlighting your greatest achievements, you will draw the reader to the accomplishments that will most impress them. Take your time documenting this information. Go back year by year, job by job, and list as many accomplishments as you can.
6. **Bold** any special skills that you possess that directly relate to pharmaceutical sales.

> *When using the bolding technique, bold face type only the most important words in the line and don't bold the entire line. If you have many achievements, bold only your best four or five. Don't go overboard on bolding; if you do, you will lose the visual impact.*

7. List in bullet format as many quantifiable accomplishments and achievements as possible. For ideas on what to document, see the number and percentages tips that follow.

8. Put your bulleted accomplishments and achievements directly under the positions in which they occurred. If you have numerous achievements and have the space, you might like to add an "Awards and Achievements" category near the top of the résumé: It's a great attention getter.

9. Use the month, as well as the year, on all positions.

10. Put your year of graduation on the résumé if you are younger than 40 years old.

11. Put your education section near the top of the résumé. Managers are looking for that four-year degree and don't want to go fishing for it.

12. Have at least three people proofread your résumé.

13. Gear your job descriptions to sales type tasks. If you have no sales experience, emphasize public speaking skills, communication skills, leadership positions, marketing experience and training skills.

14. List any special courses that you have taken that apply to this position such as Dale Carnegie courses and public speaking courses.

15. Include any professional organizations or clubs that apply (e.g. Toastmasters International).

16. Mention a couple of your hobbies or interests if you have the space. List a few on one line at the end of the résumé. This personal touch shows that you are well rounded and helps to add personality and life to the résumé. The interviewer may choose to interview you simply because you have something in common with him/her (golf is a great hobby to add: Many physicians love to golf).

LIGHTNING CHARGED PHARMACEUTICAL SALES SPECIFIC OBJECTIVES:

- Top producing sales professional seeking to obtain a challenging pharmaceutical sales position with Aventis in the central Florida area which will utilize my 15 years of healthcare and sales background to enhance sales and bottom line profits for the company.
- Enthusiastic, creative, top-performing professional with strong business acumen and healthcare background currently seeking a challenging pharmaceutical sales position with Pfizer.
- Competitive and motivated individual with six years professional experience delivering increased sales, and building relationships seeking a career in pharmaceutical sales with Solvay.
- Job target: Pharmaceutical Sales
- Licensed psychologist seeks new challenge in pharmaceutical sales with Innovex. Can offer experience in solution selling/problem solving, relationship building, and ability to interact on a professional level with healthcare professionals, coupled with a keen interest in medications, biology, anatomy, and physiology.

- Enthusiastic, hard working and creative graduate wanting to use extensive knowledge in biology and business to achieve top levels in pharmaceutical sales at Ortho-McNeil Pharmaceuticals.
- Currently seeking a pharmaceutical sales position with Novartis that will effectively utilize my public speaking, organizational and leadership skills to complement corporate image and enhance company profits.

Another layout, which I like: *(Notice the keywords)*

PHARMACEUTICAL SALES

Dynamic and results-oriented professional having a successful track record with Fortune 100 companies in consumer, medical equipment, and industrial products industries seeks a rewarding career opportunity in pharmaceutical sales.

Proven professional competencies include:

- ◆ Exceeding sales quotas and business objectives
- ◆ Improving operational effectiveness
- ◆ Maximizing profits and enhancing customer satisfaction
- ◆ Bilingual business communications (Spanish/English)

Strong decision-making, leadership and interpersonal skills

FABULOUS FILLER!
IN DESPERATE NEED OF SOME QUALITY FILLER?
RÉSUMÉ TOO SHORT?

Try these proven tips. Use any and all that apply to you and incorporate into your résumé accordingly. (Notice that the bold type really helps to sell your strong points.)

- **Self-financed 80%** of education
- **GPA 3.7** out of 4.0
- **President** of Gamma Sigma Sigma National Service Sorority
- **Worked full-time while holding full course load.**
- B.A. Degree in Communication, emphasis in **public speaking** and interpersonal communication.
- Minor in **sales and marketing**

- **Top fundraiser**
- **Resident assistant** (If you were a resident assistant while in college, you can add this as a part of your work history.)
- **Promoted two times in three years**
- Member of **Mortar Board National Honor Society** (judged on scholarship, leadership, and service)
- Graduated **Magna Cum Laude** with cumulative GPA of 3.73
- **Bilingual** (Spanish and English)

Consider adding a profile *(Great if you have limited sales experience)*

Example profile: A highly motivated professional with a winning combination of detail oriented preparation and excellent public relations skills that build partnering relationships. Aggressively gains knowledge and masters new subject areas. Works well independently or as a part of a team.

Preceptorship: List it with Pizzazz!

Have you completed a field preceptorship (when you ride for a day in the field with a representative)? If you have, it's a great addition to your résumé. Include it near the top of the résumé under the education section.

A suggestion on how you might want to document it:

Field Preceptorship: February 2004
Worked with a senior professional sales specialist in the Tucson, AZ territory. Participated in call planning, interacted with office staff, and observed effective sales call techniques. Developed a sense of the what a pharmaceutical sales representative does on a daily basis.

> **Note:** If you are having problems landing a preceptorship, ask a rep if you can "follow" them into a couple of sales calls. This will provide great insight for interviews, and, in my opinion, would still qualify as a preceptorship. (This approach avoids the hassle of the rep seeking their manager's approval to have you ride in their car, etc.).
>
> If you are friendly with a physician, you may want to ask if you can hang around his/her office for a couple of hours one day. You may meet some reps and can ask if you can sit in on one of their sales calls. This, too, is a great addition to your résumé.

IMPORTANT QUESTIONS THAT YOUR RÉSUMÉ SHOULD ANSWER:

1. How did the company benefit from your sales expertise?
2. How did you perform in comparison with your peers?
3. What were your specific sales figures ($ amount if the information is not confidential or a percentage increase)?
4. How well have you met your quota or other sales expectations?
5. Did you win any sales awards?
6. Were you rewarded with a new territory because of your performance?
7. Did you land any difficult accounts? Did you salvage any accounts that had previously been languishing?
8. Were you involved in product development or a new product launch?
9. Did you overcome serious obstacles, such as selling in poor market conditions, overcoming objections or breaking into a new market?
10. Did you establish a sales training program or teach other sales pros to improve their performance?
11. Did your dedication to customer service, impeccable follow-through and support lead to repeat business or a high number of referrals?
12. Have you led contract negotiations that resulted in a positive business deal?
13. Do you negotiate with vendors or suppliers to secure favorable pricing?
14. Have you written for any industry publications or spoken at any events or conferences?
15. Did you serve on any committees or boards or participate in special projects?

13 RÉSUMÉ DON'TS:

1. Don't go overboard on long job descriptions. Simply state what you are selling, to whom and in what territory. If it is not sales related, state what you did and with whom.
2. Don't put your cell phone number on your résumé. You don't want to be getting screened for great job while driving or worse yet, while you are with your current boss!
3. Don't use the "functional" résumé format. The "chronological" format, with your current position on top, has proven to be more effective for sales positions.
4. Don't use wordy, lengthy paragraphs.
5. Don't use the first person. Never say "I," "mine, "my," etc.
6. Don't mention an associate's degree if you have a bachelor's degree.
7. Don't leave any unexplained gaps between positions or between college and first job.
8. Don't waste space with the line "References available upon request" (it is a given and understood).

9. Don't mention marital status or age.

10. If you are running out of space, don't waste space with a separate section on "Summary of Qualifications." A good place to add some adjectives about yourself would be in the objective of your résumé.

11. Don't underline your email address.

12. Don't use a "less than professional" email address. (If you were a hiring manager, would you really take huggybear@aol.com seriously?)

13. Don't use passive language. If you use "passive voice" it suggests that this person isn't aggressive or assertive. MS Word spell check will clue you in on this. Switch the verbage to "active" mode. A small but vital change!

MAKE YOUR RÉSUMÉ MAKE AN IMPRESSION WITH NUMBERS!
(Fill in the blanks and use on your résumé and/or cover letter where appropriate.)

*Note: Pharmaceutical managers hire people
with quantifiable achievements!*

1. _____ (#) years of extensive experience in _____ and _____

2. Won _____ (#) awards for _____

3. Trained/Supervised _____ (#) full-time and _____ (#) part-time employees.

4. Recommended by _____ (a number of notable people) as a _____ (something good that they said about you) for excellent _____ (an accomplishment or skill)

5. Supervised a staff of _____ (#).

6. Recruited _____ (#) staff members in _____ (period of time), increasing overall production.

7. Sold _____ (# of products) in _____ (period of time), ranking _____ (1st, 2nd, 3rd) in sales in a company of _____ (#) employees.

8. Exceeded goals in _____ (#) years/months/days, establishing my employer as _____ (number: 1st, 2nd, 3rd) in industry.

9. Missed only _____ (#) days of work out of _____ (#) total.

10. Assisted _____ (#) (executives, supervisors, technical directors, _____ others).

MAKE YOUR RÉSUMÉ RULE THE PILE WITH PERCENTAGES!

Note: The more quantifiable achievements, the better!

1. Excellent _____ (your top proficiency) skills, which resulted in _____ (%) increase/decrease in (sales, revenues, profits, clients, expenses, costs, charges).
2. Recognized as a leader in company, using strong skills to effect a/an (%) increase in team/co-worker production.
3. Streamlined _____ (industry procedure), decreasing hours spent on task by _____ (%).
4. Used extensive _____ (several skills) to increase customer/member base by _____ (%).
5. Financed (%) of tuition/education/own business.
6. Graduated within the top _____ (%) of class.
7. Responsible for an estimated _____ (%) of employer's success in _____ (functional area/market).
8. Resolved customer relations issues, increasing customer satisfaction by _____ (%).
9. Eliminated (an industry problem), increasing productivity by _____ (%).
10. Upgraded _____ (an industry tool), resulting in _____ (%) increase in effectiveness.

RÉSUMÉ BOOSTING ACTION VERBS

(Use them to create a more powerful résumé)

Refer to this list of power verbs when you are writing your résumé. Use a select few that best describe your skills, your experience, and achievements. Be sure not to use too many: You don't want to have a résumé that looks like the sample that we just made fun of.

TIP: When describing your present job duties, use the present tense; when describing past job duties, use the past tense.

A, B — abridged, absolved, accelerated, accomplished, accounted for, achieved, acquired, acted, adapted, added, addressed, adjusted, administered, advanced, advertised, advised, aided, allocated, altered, analyzed, answered, applied, appointed, appraised, approved, arbitrated, arranged, articulated, assembled, assessed, assigned, assimilated, assisted, attained, attended, audited, augmented, authored, authorized, automated, balanced, began, bid, blended, broadened, budgeted, built

C — calculated, calibrated, cared for, carved, categorized, catalogued, chaired, changed, charted, chose, clarified, classified, coached, coded, collaborated, collated, collected, combined, communicated, compared, compiled, completed, composed, compounded, computed, conceived, conceptualized, condensed, conducted, conferred, confirmed, confronted, conserved, considered, consolidated, contracted, constructed, consulted, contacted, contracted, contributed, controlled, converted, conveyed, convinced, cooperated, coordinated, copied, corrected, corresponded, counseled, created, critiqued, customized, cut

D — debated, debugged, decided, decreased, defined, delegated, delineated, delivered, demonstrated, derived, described, designated, designed, detected, determined, developed, devised, diagnosed, differentiated, directed, disbursed, discovered, dispatched, dispensed, displayed, disproved, distributed, diversified, documented, doubled, drafted, dramatized, drew up

E — earned, edited, educated, effected, elaborated, elicited, eliminated, enabled, encouraged, enforced, engineered, enhanced, enlisted, ensured, entertained, established, estimated, evaluated, examined, exceeded, executed, exhibited, expanded, expedited, experimented, explained, explored, expressed, extended, extracted

F fabricated, facilitated, familiarized, fashioned, filed, finalized, fixed, focused, followed, forecasted, formulated, fortified, found, founded, framed, functioned as, furnished, furthered

G, H, I — gained, gathered, generated, governed, greeted, guaranteed, guided, halted, halved, handled, headed, helped, hired, hosted, identified, illustrated, implemented, improved, incorporated, increased, individualized, indoctrinated, influenced, informed, initiated, innovated, inspected, installed, instilled, instituted, instructed, insured, integrated, interacted, interpreted, intervened, interviewed, introduced, invented, invested, investigated, involved, isolated, itemized

J, L — joined, judged, justified, launched, lectured, led, lessened, listened, litigated, limited, located, logged

M, N, O — made, maintained, managed, manipulated, manufactured, marketed, marshaled, mastered, maximized, measured, mediated, memorized, merged, met, modeled, moderated, modified, molded, monitored, motivated, named, narrated, navigated, negotiated, netted, neutralized, nominated, normalized, notified, nurtured, observed, obtained, offered, offset, opened, operated, orchestrated, ordered, organized, originated, outlined, overhauled, oversaw, owned

P, Q — participated, perceived, performed, persuaded, photographed, pinpointed, pioneered, planned, predicted, prepared, prescribed, presented, presided, prevented, printed, prioritized, processed, produced, programmed, projected, promoted, proposed, protected, proved, provided, publicized, purchased, qualified, quantified, quoted

R — raised, realized, rearranged, received, recommended, reconciled, recorded, recruited, rectified, redesigned, reduced, referred, registered, regulated, rehabilitated, reinforced, related, remodeled, rendered, reorganized, repaired, replaced, replicated, reported, represented, reproduced, researched, reserved, resolved, responded, restored, restructured, retrieved, revamped, reversed, reviewed, revised, revitalized, routed

S — saved, scheduled, screened, sculptured, searched, secured, selected, served, serviced, set up, shaped, shortened, signed, simplified, simulated, sketched, smoothed, solicited, sold, solidified, solved, sparked, spearheaded, specialized, specified, speculated, spoke, sponsored, staffed, standardized, started, stimulated, streamlined, strengthened, stretched, structured, studied, submitted, succeeded, suggested, summarized, supervised, supplied, supported, surpassed, surveyed, synthesized, systemized

T — tabulated, tallied, tasted, taught, tempered, terminated, tested, testified, traced, tracked, trained, transformed, translated, transmitted, traveled, trimmed, troubleshot, turned, tutored

U, V, W — uncovered, underlined, underscored, undertook, underwrote, unearthed, unified, united, updated, upgraded, used, utilized, validated, vaulted, verified, visualized, volunteered, widened, won, worked, wrote

X, Y, Z

HOW DOES YOUR RÉSUMÉ STACK UP?

*Résumé summary provided by the sales résumé pros
at CRI (www.careerresumes.com)*

If you are in the process of writing or rewriting your résumé, you may want to use this summary to see how well it performs. Evaluate your résumé **before** you rewrite it to see which areas may need some extra tweaking. When you feel your résumé is in great shape, come back to this summary for another review. Repeat this process until you are satisfied with your score.

This is a brief summary of how a Human Resources professional would view your résumé. Max score of 10 in each column. Scores: 90–100, Excellent; 80–90, Good; less than 80, Average.

Criteria	Score
Have a clearly stated objective. The reader needs to know what you are seeking. Not having a clearly stated objective is the most common mistake seen on résumés.	
Have all contact information. List home phone number, address and e-mail. Be sure your e-mail address and your voicemail message are professional. Do not use a P.O. box.	
Have a "Profile" section, which quickly tells the reader how you stand out from your peers. Tell the reader a.) Your areas of expertise, and b.) Your overall experience. Companies are seeking specialists who also have a diverse complement of experience and skills.	
Avoid subjective statements. Avoid "outstanding, tremendous" or any other subjective verbiage that the reader may doubt. It is usually best to make (objective) statements about your actual experience.	
Verbiage in résumé is "results-orientated." Do not just list what you have done; also list the *beneficial results* of your work. Companies want to see results.	

continued on next page

Criteria	Score
Achievements are well-qualified or quantified. If you can say you were the "top sales rep" that is OK, but saying, "Top sales rep out of 35 sales reps" is more impressive.	
Projects showcase soft and technical skills. For each project, list a.) The challenge you faced; b.) The actions you took; and c.) The beneficial results of your actions. This technique enables you to showcase your soft skills and technical skills.	
Significant level of relevant key phrases. This is usually a weak point for résumés. Be sure all relevant key phrases are listed or you will miss out on interviews. Know the latest industry specific key phrases.	
The aesthetic "look" of the résumé. Is it professional looking and easy to read?	
The "oatmeal test." As a child, your mother likely told you to eat oatmeal because it would "stick with you." After reading your résumé, would it "stick with" (be remembered by) the reader? Your résumé must be memorable: According to a recent article in the *U.S. News & World Report*, Fortune 500 companies receive 400 résumés every day.	
Your Score:	

Notes: _____

_____

_____

_____

_____

_____

_____

_____

_____

_____

My opinion of the monster job boards:

In the 4 years that I have had my book and email helpline, I have gotten a lot of feedback about how people are landing pharma sales jobs. Time and again, I hear most success stories from people who have gotten out and networked their way in. I have also heard many success stories from people who have used recruiters who specialize in placing pharmaceutical pros... a very distant third option is posting on the monster job sites.

I have heard of very few candidates getting interviews by posting to a job on one of the monster sites. (Sites that are more targeted like *medzilla.com* and *hirerx.com* are better choices because they don't have as many resumes in their database.)

Think about this: Everyone posts to those monster sites. Yes, the companies use them and look for candidates that way but what are your chances? Even if your keywords are an exact match to those few that are entered by the hiring managers, the chance of your resume making the top search result pages are slim. In fact, even if you are an excellent candidate, your resume could potentially end up on page 50.

If you do want to apply to companies online, you are much better off going directly to the companies themselves. Go to their websites (see listing at back of book) and post your resume or if you have the email addresses of HR people, email it directly to them. By getting your resume directly into their own database or better yet, into their inbox, you are greatly raising your odds of success.

Yes, this can be a time consuming task, but it is well worth the effort. If you would like help distributing your resume, visit my website at *pharmaceutical-salesinterviews.com* and check out my newest time saving service: Targeted resume distribution.

E-RÉSUMÉS:
HOW TO STAY OUT OF THE RÉSUMÉ ABYSS

Have you posted your résumé online? How many responses did you get? If you weren't happy with the number of responses, you are not alone. Many online job seekers don't realize that a well-written résumé has a new set of rules that apply when going the cyberspace route.

Who is reading my e-résumé?

If you send your résumé directly to managers, a human will be reading your résumé. If you also plan to go the cyberspace route, three types of "people" will be reading it: Actually, two of them are humans, the third is a computer. When applying online or when emailing a résumé, you need to write your résumé for the three potential audiences that will be reading it: employers, executive recruiters, and résumé scanning systems.

Employers: Generally, if you apply to companies online, your résumé goes to a person in human resources. Human resources staff tend to be very overworked so think of how you might get someone's attention when they are rushed: Answer the big questions.

Questions that employers like answered on your résumé:
1. What specific job does this candidate want? Put this in the objective.
2. What is this candidate's general overall employment background?
3. What expertise or specific skills does this candidate offer?

Think of your résumé as a movie trailer. You are trying to pique your audience's interest. Answer their three top questions and leave them wanting to know more about you!

Executive Recruiters: Having a well-written résumé is critical when dealing with executive recruiters. The advice above holds true, and recruiters also want to know two more things: Where do you want to work/live (geographically), and what are your salary requirements? You will need to provide that information and the best location is in the cover letter. Don't leave them guessing: If they have to make a phone call to find out, they will probably not make the phone call.

Résumé scanning systems: Most large pharmaceutical companies (Merck, Pfizer, etc.) scan the résumés they get. Why? Because it is simple, inexpensive and efficient. This is good news for them, but may be bad news for you! Your résumé stands a good chance of getting 'lost' in their database instead of being read by a human being.

How to write a résumé for a résumé scanning system:
(This will be a separate version of the document that you will send directly to managers with this program.)

Be sure to mention **pharmaceutical industry specific keywords** in your résumé. Computers will be looking for those keywords or phrases. For example: Specifically mention pharmaceutical sales in your objective, major pharmaceutical company names, (including their own), product names, generic products, and managed care organizations, to name a few. Contrary to popular belief, you can bold or underline virtually anything in your résumé to give it "eye appeal." Use an 11 or 12 font size.

Food for thought:
Including two to three more relevant key words than your competition can help bring success vs. failure in securing an interview.

Keywords/Buzzwords:
sales representative, sales professional, district sales manager, regional sales manager, VP of sales, account executive, account manager, sales executive, sales engineer, director of sales, sales support manager, territory sales representative, territory manager, channel sales manager, manufacturer representative, technical sales, medical sales representative, pharmaceutical sales, e-business sales manager, investment representative, IT sales solution selling, relationship building, relationship selling, relationship sales, customer

service, customer relations, client relations, territory expansion, consultative sales, product marketing, negotiating and closing, channel sales, B2B/B2C, lead generation, OEMs, VARs, communication skills, new business development, sales presentations, PowerPoint, meeting and exceeding sales quotas, outside sales, inside sales, sales expansion, various drug names, specialty sales rep, hospital sales, managed care

E-résumé tips that land the interviews:

If you are planning to apply for pharmaceutical sales positions online, pay close attention. Following these simple tips can make or break your online success.

If you do not follow these guidelines,
you may be wasting your time applying!

When you post a résumé online, more often than not you are sending it to a computer.

Initially, the computer is selecting résumés based on some programmed criteria. Your résumé must impress the computer and it must speak the language of the computer. If you simply send your résumé, there is a good chance that it will not be read simply because the computer was unable to read the file or the format.

You need an e-version of your résumé to effectively get your qualifications into cyberspace. This holds true for e-mailing and for posting on résumé databases.

Helpful tip:

When emailing your résumé, always send two versions: Send one
as a Word document (or some other word-processed document)
and send a second that has been converted to ASCII.
By sending two documents, you are covering your bases.
If the company is unable to read or open your Word file,
it will be able to read your ASCII version. Professional résumé
writers can help you convert your résumé for a small fee
of approximately $25.

Be sure to mention to the recipient that you are including both versions.

How to Create an E-résumé:

The first thing that you must do is convert your résumé to ASCII format.

What is ASCII? ASCII stands for American Standard Code for Information Interchange. ASCII is a form of data that can be understood by most computers throughout the world. When you convert your résumé to this format, you don't have to worry about whether or not the recipient can open the file or read the format.

Think about how many times you've gotten an email attachment that you couldn't open. Unless it was something important, you probably deleted it.

This is exactly what happens to résumés on the employer's end. If a résumé can't be read, the job seeker won't be selected for an interview. Employers will not email you to say that they were unable to read your résumé. No second chances here!

How to convert a résumé to ASCII: Open the résumé in your word processing program (such as Word or WordPerfect) and "save as" plain text (in Word 97/2000, select File > Save As > Save as Type, choose Text Only). You may then get a prompt stating that your document "may contain features that are not compatible with text only format"— choose Yes. Then do any "clean up" necessary.

- Change bullets to asterisks or dashes.
- If columns or tables were used in the original document, make sure the text is coherent.
- Add stylistic elements to the header sections so that they stand out. A horizontal line (up to 60 characters) may be created by using a series of dashes or asterisks.
- Make sure the most important information is in the top third of the document. Hiring managers report that they often print the screen shot, not the complete résumé.
- If a résumé is longer than one page and contains contact information on the additional pages, remove this information from the ASCII version. The ASCII résumé is meant to be read on a computer screen, so there is no distinction between page numbers.
- Some screens only read 60 characters across. Set your page width accordingly. Consider this: If your résumé is in a font size that is smaller than the standard 12, when it is copied and pasted to an email, it will convert to the standard size and throw off your layout.

- Remove all tabs and where space is required, use the spacebar. Again, this can throw off your layout.
- Use spaces to separate jobs and paragraphs not tab or return bar.
- Use only keyboard symbols — No smart quotes or mathematical symbols. Remember: If it isn't on your keyboard, don't use it.
- Also be sure to save the e-mail version under a different name so that you don't overwrite your résumé.
- To post your résumé, simply open the ASCII file, use the copy command under edit on your toolbar, and then paste into your e-mail. After you have completed the conversion, send an e-mail to yourself to see how it looks.

You are now ready to enter the job-searching world of cyberspace.

SAMPLE RÉSUMÉS

HEALTHCARE PROFESSIONAL TRANSITIONING TO PHARMACEUTICAL SALES

Resume written by Marty Weitzman of www.pharmaceuticalsalesresumes.com

OBJECTIVE

Accomplished healthcare professional seeking to leverage nursing, administrative, and management experience to establish a career in Pharmaceutical Sales.

SUMMARY OF QUALIFICATIONS

A dedicated and goal oriented individual providing solid academic credentials and cross functional experience in managed care, product knowledge, training, presentations, sales, marketing, time management, organizational and process improvement. Interface effectively

EXPERIENCE

TRIAD HEALTH MGMT. SERVICES Toledo, OH   July 1996–Present
A specialty service focusing on newborns admitted to NICUs and special care nurseries. The company establishes agreements with health plans, employers, and insurers to provide extensive case management services for infants and their families.

Clinical Operations/Care Manager
- **Participate in company marketing programs; present formal presentations to groups to promote the sale and implementation of care management services to health plans and to hospital management.**
- Coordinate actions between CM's, medical directors, and clients to facilitate achievement of desired clinical and fiscal outcomes; plan, organize, oversee, and evaluate team of care managers.
- Promotes communication among health care team and serve as a liaison between families, the health plan, and providers; collaborate with client support staff to resolve customer issues.
- Collaborate with regional Account Managers in preparation of quarterly/annual analysis and reports to management of health plans and providers; contribute to the clinical and financial success of the company and complete required reports and statistics in a timely and efficient manner.
- Worked closely with Physician Advisory Board and plan medical directors in revising clinical management guidelines, reviewing case studies, presenting provider reports
- Participated on committee that successfully obtained URAC accreditation (Utilization Review Accreditation Commission).
- Represent the company as the liaison to hospital staff, providers, and members/family.
- **Increased payer ROI 143% for 2001 and 2002 in local market.**
- **Participated with specialists and plan medical directors in creating initial Clinical Management Guidelines that have since been used with neonatalogists to reduce the degree of practice variation.**
- **Assisted in development and conducted guideline education modules for hospital staff.**

LINCOLN HOME HEALTH, Columbus, OH   1991–2003
Intake Coordinator/Staff Nurse (Full Time & Per Diem)
- Coordinate/transition adult & pediatric patient for HH services per MD orders and communicated orders to field staff.
- Assisted in marketing pediatric Home Health Services to private pediatricians via phone and presentation.
- *Quarterly Employee Award.*

STONE, EDWARDS, QUINN, PA, Columbus, OH   1988–1995
Pediatric Nurse/Office Manager – Part & Full-Time

CENTURY 21 CABOTT & ASSOC., Steubenville, OH   1986–1988
Real Estate Agent – *Won quarterly prizes for securing the most listings; named top sales agent.*

EDUCATION

BSN, Cum Laude, OHIO STATE UNIVERSITY   1996
Phi Theta Kappa Society; McGovern Silver Award; Paidos President's Advisory Board

LICENSES & CERTIFICATIONS

CNPR, National Association of Pharmaceutical Sales Representatives   RN, Ohio, Illinois, Florida
BC (Pediatrics), American Nursing Credentialing Center, 1995

MEDICAL SALES EXPERIENCE TRANSITIONING TO PHARMACEUTICAL SALES

Resume written by Marty Weitzman of www.pharmaceuticalsalesresumes.com

SUMMARY OF QUALIFICATIONS

Top performing Medical Sales and Marketing professional with proven ability to drive territorial revenue growth and increase market penetration through effective business planning, presentation, relationship building, and training.

EXPERIENCE

ANDERSON SUPPLY DEPOT, SYRACUSE, NY   Jan. 2000–Present
Full Line Durable Medical Equipment (DME), Mobility, Respiratory Services and Equipment

Regional Manager, Syracuse, NY (Sept. 2002–Present)
- Charged with driving revenue growth in this under-performing region, covering a 20 county area of NY and PA. Responsible for daily operations, quality assurance, budgeting, staffing, inventory control, compliance and licensing for all regional offices; manage staff of 16.
- *Opened and managed Utica /Rochester, NY office, a new market for company; secured and set up showroom; worked closely with Sales Representative to identify and secure referral sources; achieved 2003/first year sales of $2.28M.*
- *Increased sales for three and Corning offices from $7.4M in 2002 to $8.352M in 2003, an average increase of almost 15%.*
- *Expanded total region revenues from $7.4M to $10.38M, with 2004 projected at 15% growth.*
- *Negotiated and secured contract with Utica County Hospicare for exclusive use of Anderson Supply Depot services for their patients; represented $100K in 2003 and 5% of Ithaca market with 2004 projected at $163K representing 7% of market.*
- *Developed (CHF) Congestive Heart Failure/(COPD) Chronic Obstructive Pulmonary Disease screening and educational programs utilized company-wide.*
- Instrumental in developing a direct mailing prescription service, implemented in Jan. 2004.

Office Manager/Clinical Specialist/Sales, Johnstown, NY (Jan. 2000–Aug. 2002)
- Challenged with invigorating sales in regional office with two-year record of no significant market penetration in the Corning/Elmira market; managed daily operations, provided clinical follow-up, and staff supervision.
- *Researched and targeted high potential referral sources and developed business plan to build strong referral network, including direct office visits, in-service training, and luncheons with physicians, nurses and other healthcare professionals.*
- *Grew office from 117 clients and $750K sales to over 500 clients and $2.964M respectively.*

Robert Woods Johnson Hospital, Utica, NY   Sept. 1979–Dec. 1999
**Clinical Supervisor/Clinical Instructor for the School of
Respiratory Therapy (Sept. 1983–Dec. 1999)**
- Supervised and trained up to 20 respiratory therapists, technicians, and students in Cardio-Pulmonary unit.
- *Adjunct faculty member at Syracuse University (1983 - 1988), with direct responsibility for clinical instruction in all aspects of Respiratory Therapy for A.S. Degree program.*
- *Transformed bronchoscopy services from an unorganized, poorly trained service, to a highly professional team that provided state-of-the-art-services to outpatients as well as in-patients throughout the organization;* operating room, emergency room, ICU, patient's room, and physician's office; trained members; evaluated and purchased new equipment, supplies, and techniques.
- Developed and monitored Infection Control program for department.
- Set-up and performed Quality Assurance program for department; identified and remediated deficiencies.
- Developed and improved policies and procedures.

Staff Respiratory Therapist (Jun. 1981–Aug. 1983) – Provided adult and pediatric respiratory care, arterial blood gas analysis, ventilator management, bronchoscopy, intubation, chest physical therapy, and acting shift supervisor.

Student (Sept. 1979–May 1981) – Clinical rotations through all areas of Cardiopulmonary Care and testing.

EDUCATION

B.S., Business Administration, Management, G.P.A. 3.4, Syracuse University, Syracuse, NY, 1987
A.S., Respiratory Therapy, G.P.A. 3.6, Elmira College, Elmira, NY, 1981

PROFESSIONAL ACTIVITIES & CERTIFICATIONS

Registered Respiratory Therapist, Licensed for Pennsylvania & New York, Member of National Board for Respiratory Care

PHARMACEUTICAL SALES EXPERIENCE

OBJECTIVE

Enthusiastic, hardworking sales professional seeking to obtain a challenging sales position with Sanofi Pharmaceuticals which will provide professional career growth.

EDUCATION

Rutgers College (Rutgers University)
MBA — Marketing: expected fall 2005
Delta Mu Delta member, National Honor Society in Business Administration
Fairleigh Dickinson University
BA — Economics: May 1987
Double Majors: Economics and History. Minor: Chemistry

EXPERIENCE

AMGEN
Key Accounts Representative: 2/96 to Present
Responsible for marketing and sales at key teaching, city, and government hospitals in the metropolitan area.
Emphasis on large oncology practices, AIDS centers, regional buying groups and wholesaler management.
Accomplishments include:
• **"Rookie of the Year"** in 1996 for Amgen.
• **Sales Contest Winner,** New Products for 3rd and 4th Quarter 1996.
• **Top account manager** in sales increase versus quota for 1st quarter 1997.

JOHNSON & JOHNSON (JANSSEN)
Hospital Specialty Representative: 7/93 to 2/96
Responsible for sales and marketing at major teaching hospitals in New York City.
Expanded sales volume by obtaining ten significant formulary approvals in two years.
Accomplishments include:
• **Top ranked representative in region for antifungal sales.**
• **Top 5% in region** for total sales in 1995.
• Obtained formulary contract with largest, private HMO in NY City.
• **Top 4%** in Janssen National Product Knowledge Quiz for 1995.

JOHNSON & JOHNSON (JANSSEN PHARMACEUTICA)
District Trainer and Professional Representative: 12/90 to 7/93
Responsible for marketing and sales for office-based physicians and community hospitals in New Jersey.
Accomplishments include:
• **District Representative of the Year** – 1991.
• **Number one ranking in sales** Eastern Region – 1991.
• Expanded responsibilities included: District Trainer, Interview Selection Workshop, and Safe Driving Coordinator.

HALLMARK
Territory Manager: 2/89 to 12/90
Responsible for sales of giftware to large retail chains, pharmacies, and independent stores.
Hired, trained, and supervised over 25 part-time merchandisers. Annual quota of over 2.5 million dollars in sales.
• Achieved **"excellent" annual performance** appraisal.

SKILLS

• Janssen Advanced Hospital Training Seminar, September 1993
• Janssen Advanced Selling Skills Seminar, March 1992
• Toastmasters International Member, Bergen County Chapter

RECENT COLLEGE GRADUATE

Objective:
Enthusiastic, hard working and creative graduate wanting to use an extensive knowledge in biology and business to achieve top levels in pharmaceutical sales at Ortho-McNeil Pharmaceuticals.

Education:
ELIZABETHTOWN COLLEGE, *Elizabethtown, PA*
B.S. in Biology (Finance Minor)
Cumulative **GPA 3.74**
Financed 80% of education.

Academic Honors:
Presidential Scholar, Biology Honor Society
Alpha Lambda Delta Freshman Honor Society
Delaware County **Scholar – Athlete** for 1997
Bronsdorf Award winner & **Presidential Service Nominee**

Work Experience:

MORGAN STANLEY DEAN WITTER INTERN, *Harrisburg, PA: Spring 2001*
Assisted a financial advisor with increasing his client base by publicizing through mailers and cold calling. Helped organize investment seminars.

TOTAL REHAB INTERNSHIP, *Marple, PA: Summer 1999*
Volunteer internship position at Physical Therapy Office helping patients.
Worked with physicians and learned about the needs and wants of the industry.

PAM CAPITAL REINSURANCE INTERN, *Philadelphia, PA: Summer 1998*
Responsible for closing claims after researching account history of firm. Duties also included data entry into the PAM Solar System.

CAMP INSTRUCTOR, *Wallingford, PA: Summer 1994–1997*
Worked as an assistant camp instructor teaching school age students the sport of basketball.

Activities:
Member of **Varsity Basketball** & Golf Teams
Vice President of Circle K Service Club
Attended Advanced Leadership Forum to improve interpersonal skills.
Student Government Representative, Jazz Band Member

Personal:
Expert in Microsoft Office including Word, Excel, and Power Point.
Excellent public speaker
Completed Marine Corp Marathon and raised over $2,000 for the
Leukemia and Lymphoma Society

B to B SALES EXPERIENCE

JOB TARGET: PHARMACEUTICAL SALES WITH PFIZER
WILLING TO RELOCATE

PROFILE OF STRENGTHS:

Related Experience: 7 years of direct business-to-business sales experience with proven record of landing and maintaining key accounts; **5 years of retail sales, and 2 years of nursing studies.**

Relevant Coursework: Anatomy, Physiology, Microbiology and Human Disease, Developmental Psychology, Nursing Care Child/Adult, and Psychology of the Aging.

Computer Skills: Proficient in Microsoft Office application, PowerPoint, and all graphic software.

Personality Traits: Loyal, dedicated, tenacious, self starter, positive can-do attitude, mature, poised, continually seeking self improvement, team player, creative (especially in challenging situations), flexible and versatile, enthusiastically invite constructive criticism. Combine analytical and creative abilities to resolve problems.

Organizational / Project Management: Experienced in planning all aspects of annual fundraisers, award shows, and technology/trade events.

Marketing and Promotions: Skilled and creative in preparing promotional materials.

RELATED EXPERIENCE

SPECIFICATION SALES REPRESENTATIVE, 1/98 – Present
Worldwide Papers, Lexington, Kentucky
A subsidiary of International, a Fortune 500 company, providing commercial grade printing paper and industrial packaging supplies.
Supervised Sample Department utilized by all in-house customer service, sales team, managers, and warehouse personnel. Reorganized sample area and print archives to a more self-service oriented approach. Scheduled meetings and made presentations to key decision makers with ad agencies, design houses, printers, and corporate end users. Challenged to redefine existing customer account list to include previously neglected corporate accounts and to increase high volume accounts.
Key contributions:
Increased corporate accounts by 135% over previous 2-year sales level.
Steadily increased sales 10% to 25% during tenure through a combination of new and repeat business.
Initiated contacts and was vital player in landing key accounts.
Generated 100+ sales leads annually from trade show presentations.
Successfully planned conferences, meetings, and fundraisers for design association and **increased membership 130% and 115% in successive years.**

EDUCATION
MARSHALL UNIVERSITY, Huntington, West Virginia — 1997
Bachelor or Arts — Major: Graphic Design — G.P.A. 3.3
Minors: Nursing, Biology, and Psychology

TRAINING
Attended annual sales rep meetings
Representative presenters included Michael St. Lawrence, author of *If You're Not Selling, You're Being Outsold*
Avid reader and student of sales training and motivational books by Zig Ziglar, Tony Robbins, Dale Carnegie, Stephen Covey, and others well known in the field.

*Résumé written by Lois Jobe of DynamicSalesRésumés.com

Sales Experience Transitioning to Pharmaceutical Sales

OBJECTIVE
To transition successful sales, marketing, and business development skills to a career in Pharmaceutical Sales.

SUMMARY OF QUALIFICATIONS
Goal and results-oriented professional with proven ability to drive revenue growth in highly competitive markets. A strong relationship builder with excellent individual and group presentation skills. Demonstrates broad strengths in:

New Business Development • Solutions Selling • Product Rollouts
Account Management • Product & Sales Training • Negotiations

EXPERIENCE
ANDERSON GLASS TINTING, Pasadena, CA • 6/98 – present
Glass Treatment Company Providing Ultra Violet Protection
Head of Sales & Marketing, Cofounder
• Formulated and executed marketing and advertising strategies that captured significant market share in high-end housing market.
• **Fostered and established strong referral network; maintain active customer base of 400 homebuilders, contractors, property owners, healthcare, and educational institutions.**
• Developed and implemented presentation techniques capitalizing on product knowledge and cost-benefits analysis predicated on protecting valuables from deterioration (artwork and furnishings) caused by ultra violet radiation and reduction in electric consumption through reduced air conditioning requirements.

FEDERATED NETWORK SYSTEMS, Pasadena, CA • 10/95 – 6/98
Start-Up Telecommunications Component & Software Company
Sales Representative
• Successfully presented and sold telecommunications interface cards and software to VARS and telecomm companies selling into the small business market.
• Introduced focus group concept to company that was instrumental in penetrating PC-based small office market; enabled company to create more user-friendly equipment and programs.
• Presented at PC User Groups throughout California, including a Pasadena PC Users conference attended by over 2400 members.
• Represented company at COMDEX, the Computer Industry's premier trade show.
• Trained new Sales representatives in product knowledge, sales, and presentation techniques.
• **Played key role in propelling company from $500K to $6M in less than three years.**
• **Ranked as #1 sales representative of 8, generating almost 22% ($1.4M) of company's total business.**

UNITED CARPET BROKERS, Pasadena, CA • 6/93 – 10/95
Commercial Flooring
Sales Representative
Inside Sales/ Service Representative (6/93 – 12/93)
• Successfully sold a wide range of hard surface and resilient flooring to hospitals, school districts, local governments, property managers, and contractors.
• Gave direct presentations; prepared bids and negotiated sale on projects valued at up to $750K
• *Attained recognition as company's top Sales Representative; increased Property Management sales 75%.*

EDUCATION
BA, Political Science, UCLA, Los Angeles, CA, 1993
Received Multiple Academic Scholarships, Editor of School Newspaper

LANGUAGES
• Conversational German, Computer Literate

Résumé written by Marty Weitzman

Transitioning to Sales

2225 Maple Drive • Columbus, OH 23602
Home (555) 555-5555 • Work (555) 555-5555
Email: slhobbitt@net.com

LICENSED PHARMACIST seeks new challenge in pharmaceutical sales that can benefit from expertise and experience interacting on a professional level with health care professionals, coupled with pharmacy management experience, scientific background, and excellent organizational and communication skills.

Highlights of Qualifications

Effectively interact with physicians, office staff, and patients on a daily basis; self assured speaking style.

Strong grasp of drugs' effects — accustomed to memorizing large amounts of information and being able to answer questions about drugs.

Flexible and adaptable with ability to "think on my feet" and handle unexpected pharmacy or patient problems.

Excellent organizational and planning skills — completely reorganized pharmacy to improve efficiency and to track inventory more accurately.

Computer Skills: Proficient in Microsoft Word and Excel and well versed in PowerPoint.

Personality Traits: Enthusiastic … very friendly … articulate and communicate well … good team player … never procrastinate … very productive and efficient … well rounded … self disciplined and work well alone and unsupervised … possess strong ethics … loyal.

Professional Experience

PHARMOR, Columbus, Ohio   February 2000 – Present
Pharmacy Manager
Hired to manage pharmacy operations and staff of 4. Perform drug utilization review to check for side effects, contraindications, and drug interactions. Counsel patients on prescription and non-prescription drugs. Maintain pharmacy inventory of drugs and supplies. Resolve billing problems with insurance companies, and effectively evaluate and rectify prescription discrepancies with physicians or transfer issues with out-of-state pharmacies.

Contributions:
Improved sales by 11% through improved customer service and by revamping operational management of pharmacy and staff.
Turned around pharmacy with declining sales; reclaimed disgruntled customers, and rebuilt customer loyalty.

PHARMOR , Columbus, Ohio   June 1998 – January 2000
Pharmacy Intern

MAJOR PHARMACY, Athens, Ohio   July 1995 – May 1998
Pharmacy Technician

Education

The Ohio State University, Columbus, Ohio — May 1997
PharmD (Doctor of Pharmacy) — May 1999 — GPA 3.2

Ohio University, Athens, Ohio — May 1994
Bachelor of Science — Major: Biology

*Résumé written by Lois Jobe of DynamicSalesRésumés.com

Section 3:
Cover Letters That Outdistance The Herd!

▷ ▷ ▷

COVER LETTERS THAT OUTDISTANCE THE HERD!

Most people detest the task of writing cover letters. The majority of pharmaceutical job seekers copy a sample cover letter from a cover letter reference book and mail it in with their resume. There are two problems with this:

1. **Everyone else copies a similar letter.**

2. **The cover letters that are shown in many of these books are generic and do not convey the information that pharmaceutical sales managers are looking for.**

The reality is that pharmaceutical managers are tired of reading the same canned material over and over. Everyone seems to begin his or her letter with "This letter is in response to your advertisement in the _____ paper."

A better alternative might be to begin your letter with: "When I read your ad in Sunday's newspaper, I knew this job at Pfizer was the one for me!" This approach shows enthusiasm, personality, and originality — all traits that managers look for.

Put some thought into your cover letters. Come up with content that you will use over and over again. As you find out about openings, edit them and personalize them. Mention specific company names and make it sound as if this is the only cover letter you have written and that this is the only job you want!

COVER LETTER DO'S AND DON'TS:

As much as we would like to avoid it, resumes must be accompanied by a cover letter. A cover letter is a required tool to promote your candidacy.

DO:
- Personalize your cover letter. Avoid "To whom it may concern" or "Dear Sir/Madam" whenever possible. If you follow this program, you should have a name for each letter.
- Make your cover letter an addendum to the resume, not a rewrite of the resume itself.
- Be brief and to the point. The person reading your resume is probably very busy and has little interest in reading a novel.

- Highlight pertinent information and provide relevant data that may not be covered in your resume. If you find that a manager requires certain skills or experience that you have, this is the place to tout it.
- Be positive and confident. Let them know that you believe in yourself and can be a valuable asset to the company.
- Be sure to tell them where and when to reach you.
- Let them know that if you don't hear from them by a certain date, you will be following up with a call.
- Match the cover letter and envelopes to the resume. It makes a better presentation.
- Proofread, proofread, proofread!

DON'T:
- Don't rewrite your resume in your cover letter.
- Don't bore the reader. Be brief and not too wordy.
- Don't handwrite the letter.
- Don't use first names; Mr. or Ms. is more appropriate.
- Don't forget to sign the letter.
- Don't use your company email address.

BASIC COMPONENTS OF IMPRESSIVE COVER LETTERS

Format:
The cover letter should be written in the typical "business letter" format. It should be written on the same stationary and in the same font as the resume.

First Paragraph:
The first line should be an attention getter. The first paragraph should be no more than three sentences long, and should accomplish the following:
1. Introduce yourself
2. Explain why you're applying. (e.g., referred from a friend, responding to an advertisement, etc.)
3. Tell them where you want to work geographically.

Second / Third Paragraph(s):

Use the second and/or third paragraphs to briefly highlight your past educational and professional experiences/qualifications. Draw examples of your experience which apply or correlate directly to pharmaceutical sales. Use keywords and terms that apply to pharmaceutical sales or to the ad.

Examples of keywords:
- sales experience
- sales success
- teamwork/team-player
- results-oriented
- exceeded marketshare goals
- exceeded sales goals
- medical experience
- pharmacy experience
- clinical experience
- build relationships

Final Paragraph:

State that you would like to meet with them in person. Give them your contact information so they can easily reach you. Set a time limit. Tell them that you are eagerly awaiting their response and will follow up in a week or so.

Sample Cover Letter #1

JULIE A. DOE
Street Address
Any Town, Any State 44352
Telephone: (212) 343-6675
juliedoe@aol.com

December 1, 2004

Mr. Smith, District Manager
Novartis Pharmaceuticals
124 E. Kentucky Ave.
Any City, State 48573

Dear Mr. Smith:

I have met with Jake Lane, your representative in the central New Jersey territory. He has informed me that you have an immediate opening for a pharmaceutical sales representative in the northern New Jersey territory and suggested that I forward my resume to you for consideration. Please regard this letter as my formal application.

I have more than seven years experience in the sales and marketing field, and three years experience as an RN. Throughout my sales and marketing career I won top sales awards, and trained other sales representatives on specific sales techniques to increase their sales. I enjoy working with the public, demonstrating products, and educating others in their uses. I believe I would excel in pharmaceutical sales because I find sales a challenging and rewarding career. In addition, my nursing background offers an advantage in better understanding the products that I would sell.

May I arrange an interview to further discuss my qualifications in person? I am available for an interview at a mutually convenient time and can be reached at 212.343.6675. I am looking forward to meeting you and will follow up in a week or two.

Thank you for your time and consideration.

Sincerely,
Julie A. Doe

Sample cover letter #2:
(Recent college graduate)

March, 2004

Mr. Morgan
District Sales Manager
Ortho-McNeil Pharmaceuticals
234 Center Street
Philadelphia, PA 33454

Dear Mr. Morgan,

Please accept this letter and attached resume as an application for a sales position for the opening in your Philadelphia territory. I come highly recommended by Glen Markos, your top sales representative in the Cherry Hill territory.

Working for Ortho-McNeil will fulfill three of my employment goals: working for a successful and distinguished company, combining my interest in finance and biology, and being part of a team that helps others lead healthier lives. The pharmaceutical and biological industry is expanding every day with new scientific discoveries and healthcare products. I will bring skills helping Ortho McNeil continue to sell cutting edge products in this competitive market.

I am a self-motivated, diligent individual who wants a career in the pharmaceutical industry, specifically in sales. As a biology major and finance minor, I have gained vast knowledge in both fields while maintaining a GPA of 3.74.

I enjoy working with a diverse team of people in an energetic, fast paced environment. I thrive in an atmosphere of multiple tasks, as demonstrated by my ability to balance a full schedule while playing on the men's varsity basketball team and serving as vice president of the Circle K Club. I look forward to challenges and strive to meet personal goals within each additional task.

I can be reached either during the day or evening by calling 999.222.4444 or by email at John@eliz.edu.com. Thank you for your consideration. I am looking forward to meeting with you.

Sincerely,
John Doe

Sample Cover Letter #3

Susan Smith

10524 North Pointe Court   Home 502-426-3402
Louisville, KY 40241   Mobile 502-540-2332
Email: ssmith@msn.com

May 4, 2004

Mr. Hoban, District Manager
Glaxo Smith Kline
453 South Carlyle St.
San Diego, CA 92104

Re: Pharmaceutical Sales Position

Dear Mr. Hoban,

I am in hot pursuit of a pharmaceutical sales position with Glaxo Smith Kline. I am eager to work in an industry that will allow me to utilize my combined talents, education, and creativity at maximum potential for the benefit of all concerned. Therefore, I want to provide you with a brief overview of my particular background to show you what an excellent addition I will make to your team. Upon reviewing my attached résumé, you will find an excellent history of improving sales margins, communication skills, creativity, time management and successful cost containment, plus a BA in Design with minors in Nursing, Biology, and Psychology. Couple these with an abundance of energy and desire to be the best, and you have a unique and winning combination. Although I have lived in the San Diego area for thirteen years, know it well, and truly love it here, I am not opposed to relocating—if it would mean the perfect career.

Currently, I am working full time as an interior designer and sales consultant in the import and contemporary furniture community. After hours, I work independently providing outsource work for a local designer. I create package design and provide sales presentations for these innovative ideas to a major San Diego-based industry. I also have had the opportunity for the first time to do volunteer work for some of my favorite causes. Although I have a great love for the work I am

continued on next page

(continued from previous page)

presently doing, I am most excited about the prospects of the next step to be taken in my ever-evolving creative sales career, and pharmaceutical sales seems a perfect fit for what I have to offer.

My enthusiasm for both Arts and Science made up my Bachelor's degree at Marshall University in 1989. Before graduating, I made my way by working at a Huntington-based interior decorating company and picked up freelance graphic design work. After graduation, I applied part of my education to a Graphic Design career in Louisville for seven years. To improve upon my potential, I tackled the world of sales and specifications in 1996 with Nationwide Papers. The merger of our parent company, Champion International, with International Papers at the end of 2000 afforded me an opportunity to explore new avenues freely and enthusiastically, and I proved I can be successful in a sales environment.

I would greatly appreciate an opportunity to speak with you in person and to prove that I can make an outstanding addition to your sales team. My business associates and clients will tell you that I have an undisputed reputation for being quite loyal to my employers, and I offer that commitment with the certainty that the next direction I take will be the best, most interesting, and most profitable one, yet!

Again, thanks for your time and consideration.

Sincerely,
Susan C. Smith

Can we talk "creative" cover letter?
(Inventive cover letter sample)

The following is an attention-getting cover letter that was written by one of my customers and reprinted with his permission.

...Breaking News: Gary Lewis reportedly seeking position as pharmaceutical sales representative with 'company name.'

Dear *'hiring manager's name,'*

San Diego, CA. — It has recently been confirmed that Gary Lewis has entered the job market for a pharmaceutical sales position. In an interview last Wednesday, Mr. Lewis said that though he is aware that the competitive nature of breaking into pharmaceutical sales may require taking a position with a lesser-known company, he has his sights set on working for *'company name.'*

Lewis, a Los Angeles native who has made his home in San Diego for the past four years, stated that *'company name'* is the most attractive company to him because *'discuss a few pertinent and distinguishing reasons in this paragraph.'*

When asked what he brings to the proverbial table, Lewis had this to say: *"I am confident that I would be perceived as a polished, well-spoken individual by anybody I come in contact with. As far as sales experience goes, I've sold [mortgage] insurance policies to consumers and have, most recently, managed e-business accounts worth millions of dollars, so I don't feel that I lack anything in this area. What I want to emphasize though is that I feel my strong suit is in the rapport that I am able to develop with a wide variety of people. Relationship building has always come naturally to me. I think this is due in large part to the fact that I place myself in others' shoes and treat them the way I would want to be treated. I think my genuineness, professionalism, and integrity is apparent to those that I deal with. In fact, I've received two letters of appreciation for the outstanding level of service I provided to clients, both unsolicited I might add, as well as a letter of recognition from the company's vice president. I have also survived seven layoffs at my current company by proving myself to be a valuable asset and by becoming so well versed in the technical knowledge of the company's product that I am regarded as a product expert."*

(continued on next page)

(continued from previous page)

Lewis added that his familiarity with the various drug names, the ailments they treat, their side effects, and the companies that make them give him a competitive advantage over most other candidates looking to enter the field of pharmaceutical sales.

The interview last Wednesday concluded with Mr. Lewis stating, *"The opportunity to join an organization whose business it is to mitigate, if not completely alleviate, the symptoms of so many mental and/or physical conditions is exciting to me. I don't just want to match a sales quota for the company I work for. I want to far exceed it, if not shatter it, because that would mean that I'm helping my company in two obvious ways. First, the more people that use the drugs my company makes the more people will benefit from them. Second, the more people that use the drugs my company makes the more money I can make my company, thus enabling them to continue researching and producing even more beneficial drugs. I know I have what it takes to be a successful pharmaceutical sales representative. It's just a matter of a district manager and others involved in the hiring process giving me a chance to execute. Hopefully, my attributes and goals are what companies are looking for."*

Gary Lewis can be reached at 123.456.7890 during the daytime and at 222.333.4444 during the evenings. His email address is *lewis@aol.com*. A phone and/or face-to-face interview are welcomed.

Sincerely,
Gary Lewis

Section 4:
Pharmaceutical Sales: 3 Scenarios Of A Typical Day!

▷ ▷ ▷

PHARMACEUTICAL SALES: THREE SCENARIOS OF A TYPICAL DAY

Any insight you have about a typical day in the field is a big plus for your interviews. By having this information, you can show managers you know what the job entails and that you are the best candidate for the job.

The best way to find out what a typical day involves is through a preceptorship. If you have followed this program, you have gotten to know quite a few pharmaceutical reps so ask them if they would allow you to accompany them.

Since a preceptorship is not always possible, the following are three different "typical day" scenarios to help you better envision what a pharmaceutical rep does each day.

What is a typical day for a pharmaceutical sales representative?

Pharmaceutical representatives meet with physicians through pre-set appointments and through cold calls. During these calls, the representative will present information about their products. An average day will include eight to ten office-based sales calls. The goal during the call is to see the physician or physicians who practice there, build rapport with office staff, and check sample inventory. Depending on the company, the rep may also be required to do a pharmacy call or two.

Typical day according to Corey Nahman, pharmaceutical representative:

CN: One of the nice things about being a rep is that each day is different. Here's what a typical Friday is like for me:

I start about 7:45 a.m. and get home about 6 p.m. Fridays are always the busiest and most productive in my territory because on Fridays there is a weekly medical meeting called "grand rounds" at a large institution in my area.

Daily Planner

7:45 a.m. — Attend grand rounds at the hospital early in the morning to meet my customers for a coffee and bagel and some friendly lobbying. I might work the room, making pseudo-appointments for later in the day.

10 a.m.— Visit the hospital outpatient clinic to increase demand for my products with the residents and other house staff.

10:30 a.m. — Call on a couple of pharmacies to see how well my products are selling and see if any new doctors have moved into town.

11 a.m. — Call on a local HMO and "twist some arms" in a polite manner, of course.

1 p.m. — Take a client out to lunch or bring in lunch for a group of doctors.

2 p.m.–5:30 p.m. — Call on some of the doctors I saw at the hospital at their private offices.

I may also squeeze in a meeting with my colleagues to work on selling strategies and share marketing intelligence.

When I get home I do my expense report and any other paperwork that is due, pack my trunk with samples and goodies for the following week and check my sample inventory to make sure that it is accurate and up-to-date."

What is a typical day like at Bayer?

Rep: "A typical day starts at around 8 a.m. because I like to see as many GP's (general practitioners) as I can. This is usually about four or five a day and then a number of hospital folk in the afternoon. I will also probably see practice managers, dispensers, pharmacists and nurses. There may also be lunchtime or evening meetings, which I arrange with key customers.

The case I make for my products varies depending on what I have discovered about that customer's particular needs. I may be convincing a doctor of the clinical benefits of the product or even how the product can save money, which could mean that they are able to help more patients who need treatment. This may involve making a presentation to a group of customers and then facilitating a discussion afterwards.

There is a real buzz when I get agreement from a doctor to use my product. However, it is not just the major switches that give me that buzz. It can be something like seeing my product on a pharmacy shelf for the first time or even gaining an appointment with a difficult to see doctor!

If I were to sum it up it would be: Hard work, long hours, fantastic challenges and great fun! Recognition is an even better buzz than reward!"

What is a typical day like in a flex-time pharmaceutical sales position?

CP: "I work for DJ Pharma, Inc., which is a unique company because it hires both full-time and flex-time staff. Because I have two kids, I usually work three days a week. On those days, I drive around one of the towns in my territory and generally try to see about 10 doctors. I may spend as long as 10 minutes with a doctor, or I may get only one minute. I bring antibiotics samples, as well as clinical studies or some sort of presentation piece. I go in with fresh information every time so I can add value to the doctor's practice. It's a job that requires a lot of discipline, and it can be very rewarding. When it's a beautiful day, I love my job; when it's pouring rain or snowing, it's not so great."

> **Note:** An average rep during an average day spends approximately 30–60 minutes making sales presentations. The remainder of the day is spent preparing for calls, driving to and from calls, making small talk with office staff, stocking samples, and waiting in doctors' offices to see the physicians.

Section 5:

Interviewing: How To Toot Your Horn The Pharmaceutical Sales Way!

▷ ▷ ▷

INTERVIEWING:
(HOW TO TOOT YOUR HORN
THE PHARMACEUTICAL SALES WAY!)

The big questions about the interview process itself:

- What is the interview process like?
- I just had a phone interview, what comes next?
- How long will I have to wait for the next interview?
- How long should I wait to follow up?
- How many interviews will I have before I get an offer?
- It's been a month, when is this interview process going to end?

In an effort to come up with helpful information on what to expect while interviewing, **I interviewed the interviewees!**

I asked questions including:
- How long did you wait between interviews?
- How many interviews did you have until you got the offer?
- Who did you interview with?

Because I got so many different answers from people who had been through the interview process, I have no set in stone, official, what to expect, advice.

No two companies are alike. Some companies leave the process entirely up to the district manager while others rely on human resources personnel. Still others use a different protocol depending on how many people they are hiring. Often, a major expansion is initially handled by human resources personnel, but then again, not always. (These are not the answer that you were looking for are they?)

Unfortunately, I have no "expect this when interviewing" answer for you. The challenge is that I feel obligated to give you some information (after all, this is a "how to" book), so here goes!

General interview information to consider:

1. Most pharmaceutical sales interviews start with a phone interview. Most of the time you will hang up the phone after interviewing and not know for a few days if you are continuing on to a face-to-face interview. You can ask for a face-to-face during the phone interview but don't expect to get one on the spot.

2. The first face-to-face interview is usually with the district manager. Depending on the manager, you may be one of 30 or one of three being interviewed. Some managers love to interview and others prefer to keep the candidate list to a minimum. Always ask for another interview when the first face-to-face is over, but don't expect to get one on the spot. (Some companies hire outside firms to do their phone screening).

3. A manager will often offer a second round of face-to-face interviews to condense the candidate list. This interview can occur anywhere from a day to two months after the initial phone interview. Managers often travel a lot and there can be lag time between interviews. If there is lag time, be sure to keep in touch during the interim: You don't want them to forget about you and you want to show your continued interest in the position.

4. The next step is usually the "ride with" (you spend a day in the field with one of the star reps in the district). At this point, the field is usually narrowed to one or two other candidates. Keep in mind that the rep you are riding with will be reporting back with blow-by-blow details of your day together so be on your best behavior!

TIPS FOR A "RIDE WITH" DAY: PRECEPTORSHIP

- Smile a lot.
- Make a new friend!
- Dress your best (conservative dark suit).
- Don't badmouth your current boss.
- Be positive and enthusiastic.
- Interact with the office staff when appropriate, say hello, small talk, etc. but don't overdo it. You don't want to distract from what the rep is there to do.
- Don't ask questions like "What time do you cut out of here on Friday afternoons?"
- Do ask some questions about the district manager. You will want to know what it will take to make the final cut. Find out what the manager is looking for and who the competition is.

- Relax, be yourself, and have fun! There is really nothing special to do to prepare for this day. Get as much out of it as you can and add this preceptorship to your résumé as soon as you get back home.
- Formally thank the rep for his or her time and information and get it to them ASAP!

5. Usually, the final step in the interview process is when the interviewee meets again with the district manager and also with the regional manager. This interview is usually a formality to get the stamp of approval from the regional manager. Unless you really goof up, you usually have the job in the bag. An offer may or may not come during the interview. Sometimes the offer comes contingent upon passing drug and background checks.

TIPS TO FUEL A FABULOUS PHONE INTERVIEW

The Phone Interview:

The phone interview may be your most difficult interview because you will usually have a short amount of time to make a good impression. You also don't have the advantage of meeting the person so your good eye contact will not help in this case.

With phone interviews, best personality wins. If you got the call, you have what it takes on paper. The caller is now in the screening process and wants to find out if you can hold a conversation with someone. The caller is also looking for energy and enthusiasm so let it show through in your voice. Be prepared to answer questions and also be prepared to let your personality shine. Have fun and relax! Be sure to ask for a face-to-face interview before hanging up and save the caller's phone number for follow-up.

What can I expect?

There are so many pharmaceutical companies that it is difficult to predict what questions may be asked during a phone interview. In some instances, the manager is not the one who is making the phone call. Sometimes, human resources personnel make the call: this is often the case if a company is going through a major expansion. If you are getting a call after following this program, the call will more than likely be directly from the district manager.

Again, the questions are difficult to predict because every manager is different. As a rule, however, you can expect to be asked questions that are intended to screen out candidates and save the manager precious time.

Some screening questions that you may encounter during the phone interview:

Why are you looking for a pharmaceutical sales position?

The caller is making sure you have a good idea of what the job entails and that you want pharmaceutical sales specifically. If you answer that any sales job will do, you may lose your chance to continue on in the interview process. Managers want to hire people who are eager for pharmaceutical sales and only pharmaceutical sales.

What is your salary at your current job?

Surprisingly enough, this is the question that eliminates the majority of candidates over the phone. If you are making a substantial salary now and are willing to take a pay cut to pursue a pharmaceutical sales career, most managers, especially those in human resources, won't allow you to continue on in the interview process.

Many people have the misperception that they can start out with a poor performing territory and turn it into a big commission earner in no time. The reality is that it takes time to turn a territory around if it is underperforming: Sometimes it can take up to a year to see the results of hard work. Relationships have to be built with customers and relationship building takes time. Most managers would prefer to hire someone with a salary that is comparable to what they have to offer. It makes good business sense.

> **Suggestion:** If you are making a good salary in your current position and you are asked what you are earning, give only your base salary information. Tell the manager that you are well aware of what pharmaceutical reps make and tell them that you are prepared to work for a similar salary. FYI, pharmaceutical sales starting salaries range from 40–60K plus commission/bonuses. Some companies offer higher salaries in lieu of large commissions. Most companies pay quarterly commissions; some offer an end-of-year bonus.

Are you available for overnight travel?

If you want to work as a pharmaceutical representative, no matter what the company, some overnight travel will be required. Smaller, more urban territories usually require very little overnight travel. Regardless of the geography of the territory, be prepared to spend some overnights in hotels for regional sales meetings, district meetings, national sales meetings and sales training. Initial training can be several weeks at a time at the corporate headquarters. Meetings are usually two to three nights in duration, usually quarterly.

Are you interviewing with any other companies?

I have gotten several emails verifying that this question was asked during the phone interview and have been asked how the candidate should have answered the question. My answer is to tell the truth.

I don't know what managers would be looking for with this question but they like to ask it. Is there a best way to answer? Would the manager be impressed if you had several other interviews lined up or would they think that you aren't interested in their company specifically? I don't know. Just don't make something up to make yourself look good because it may backfire on you.

FYI...

Some companies like to get into the in-depth interviewing on the phone. Be prepared to answer situational questions on the phone as well as the screening questions. See the situational sample questions later in this chapter for help.

Here is a situational question that a manager from Pfizer asked one of my customers during her phone interview:

How would you run your territory if it were your first week on the job?

A good answer might be: I am a very organized person. I truly believe that the more organized a person is, the more professional they come across to their customers. My first task that week would be to get organized. I would sort thru my materials and set up my home office. I would organize my sales aids so that I am ready to sell when I make my way to the doctors' offices. I'd organize my trunk with ample supplies of samples and support materials and I would plan out my calls based on geography and sales potential. Once I felt that I had everything in order, I would head out and try my best to not get lost and see as many doctors as I could.

DO YOUR HOMEWORK!
(DO IT BEFORE THE PHONE INTERVIEW)

Research the company:

The more you know about a company and their products, the better you will do overall. People who have done their research impress managers. Not doing your homework gives managers the impression that you are not motivated to work for them or for their company. If you snooze, you lose! There is no second chance in this business.

Be sure to know the following:

Refer to the resource page at the back of this guidebook for help with gathering this information.

- Corporate headquarters locations.
- Products — a **basic** knowledge of what you will be promoting (names and indications will usually suffice). Don't worry about all the package insert information.
- Who their customers are (family practitioners, pulmonologists, ENTs, etc.)
- History.
- Recent news.
- Competitors (again, you won't need to know too many details. A few product brand names will suffice).
- Financial news.

Tip: Bring a copy of the information you have compiled about the company to the interview. Managers will be impressed by the fact that you are well-prepared.

> If you really want to impress your interviewer, bring along some copies of the companys' current journal advertisements. Find them in the *New England Journal of Medicine* and the *Journal of the American Medical Association (JAMA)*. You will impress the managers with this information in hand and you will also be better prepared for your interview. By looking at their journal ads, you will know which products they are currently promoting and you will also see, in print, their marketing messages.

HABITS OF HIGHLY EFFECTIVE FACE-TO-FACE INTERVIEWEES:

- Practice, practice, practice answers to common and more difficult questions.
- Prepare a list of questions to ask.
- Bring several copies of your résumé, a list of references, and a professional looking brag book (see the brag book information in this guidebook).
- Dress your absolute best.
- Dress conservatively (dark blue is always a good choice).
- Bring a pen and notepad to jot down information after the interview but don't take notes during the interview.

During the Interview:
(When all is said and done, best personality wins!)

- **You must be energetic, friendly, and enthusiastic!** This is the most important tip from this section! If you are not enthusiastic, no matter how well you answer the questions, you will not land the job. Enthusiasm sells!
- Shake hands firmly!
- Make eye contact.
- Establish rapport. Make a friend. Your interviewer wants to find out if you are someone he or she will enjoy working with.
- Laugh and smile (when appropriate).
- Be a good listener.
- Convey your drive and dedication.
- Don't lie.
- Don't say anything negative about a previous employer.
- Don't ask salary questions during the first interview.
- Be yourself. Have fun and relax!

Smart questions to ask your interviewer:

Your goal is to show genuine interest in the company, the position, and the interviewer. You don't want to appear to be asking questions just for the sake of asking them. Keep in mind that you will need to ask something. Having nothing to ask makes you appear passive and not interested in the position.

1. Ask about the competitive environment as well as the goals of the organization and management.
2. Ask what skills the interviewer considers to be the most important for the position.
3. Ask the interviewer if he or she sees a gap in your skills. If a gap is identified in your skills, this gives you an opportunity to identify the skills that you possess which you haven't already talked about in the interview.
4. Ask again about a gap in your skills. If the answer is no, **close,** and ask for the next interview. Managers always like interviewees to ask for another interview. Closing is what sales is all about! Good closers make excellent salespeople.

Additional information that you might like to gather from your interviewer:

• Detailed description of position (if you don't already know).
• Reason position is available.
• Territory status and history.
• Anticipated training program.
• Realistic earnings potential of successful salespeople. Don't bring this up on your first interview.
• Company growth plans, market share, competitors.
• Why and when did the interviewer join the company?

Don't forget to ask for the interviewer's card and email address and follow up immediately with a thank-you note. (Refer to the "Terrific, Timesaving, Templates" section of the book for help.)

BREAKING THE ICE:

The key to starting your interview out well is to break the ice. Having some good icebreaker questions to ask helps you make a good first impression and sets the tone for the interview. Small talk gives the interviewer an opportunity to get a feel for your personality and also gives you an idea of his/her personality. Most importantly, it gives you time to become acquainted and ease any tension and anxiety you may be feeling as you begin the interview.

Furthermore, taking the time to break the ice is important because it is a skill you will use all of the time when presenting to doctors. By showing your interviewer that you are good at breaking the ice, they will be able to envision you doing the same as you call on doctors.

Be sure to ask only questions that the interviewer will be happy to answer and **don't ask all of them.** Select those you feel will be the most appropriate for your situation and ask only as many as you see fit. You **do** want to get on to the interview.

Some ice breaking questions:
(Some are simply statements that get a conversation going)
- What is your position at the company? (If you don't know)
- How long have you been with the company?
- How long are you in town?
- If from out of town, "Have you had a chance to get out to any good restaurants/see any of the sites?"
- Comments about the weather.
- Statements about your trip over to the interview destination. For example, "What an easy trip. The directions were great!" Be positive: If you got lost for an hour and thought that the directions were horrific, don't tell them! Smile at all times, regardless of how you really feel.

Are you the ideal candidate?
To help prepare for the interview, it is important to think about it from the perspective of the interviewer. If you have gotten this interview from a rep referral, you probably have a good idea of the type of person that the interviewer would like to hire.

The interviewer is looking to see how you will stack up against the other interviewees in these areas:

Desire/energy: Are you an energetic person who gets up and does things with enthusiasm? Are you the type of person who wants to get ahead, who'll increase sales? This enthusiasm thing is coming up first again: It's important!

Confidence/determination: Are you a relaxed, friendly yet confident person? Someone who'll be able to get along with others and someone who'll stick to a task until it is done?

Independent: The interviewer is looking for someone who can be a team player and follow the directions of his manager combined with the maturity to be able to work unsupervised and direct and motivate him/herself. The manager is looking to see if you have this balance.

Motivation: Are you the type of person who wants to do well? To get ahead? To be creative and innovative and build sales?

Power of communication: Do you have the ability to mix with and get along with people by communicating clearly and effectively? Will you be able to make effective sales calls with outstanding communication skills?

Likeability: Are you a friendly person and easy to get along with? Someone who will add to their existing team and not disrupt it? Managers often hire people that they like and feel comfortable with over someone with more experience.

Reliability: Do you seem honest and reliable — someone who will do an honest day's work? Someone who is straightforward and has enough respect and pride in themselves to always want to do a good job?

Honesty: Do you seem to be an honest, trustworthy person? Someone whom they can have full confidence in?

Dedication: Do you seem hardworking and dedicated? Someone who starts a project and finishes it? Someone who won't complain and look for excuses to cover up failures?

Keys To Good Interview Answers:

1. Always back your interview answers up with personal real life examples. Don't just say, "I can do this and I can do that." (Your brag book will come in handy as backup.)
2. For every skill you mention, recall an incident when you successfully applied that skill.
3. Don't just say, "Yes I can!" Explain how you will do it and why you will be good at it.
4. Your answers to interview questions should always answer the question, **"But how?"** For example, don't just say, "Yes, I can absolutely increase sales! I just know that I have what it takes to make it in this business!" Show them **how** you can do it!

RELAX DURING THE INTERVIEW! BE YOURSELF!

When interviewing for pharmaceutical sales positions, you want the interview to be as conversational as possible. One of your main goals while interviewing is to "be yourself." You want to answer questions in a way that displays your enthusiasm for the job, your belief in yourself and what you can offer the company.

The job candidate who is chosen isn't necessarily the one with the most experience. In sales, the interviewee with the best personality usually lands the job. You want your personality to shine during the interview: Relax yourself and keep in mind that the person doing the interviewing was probably in your shoes not long ago. Think of the interviewer as your peer, someone you are having a conversation with as opposed to being "interviewed" by. If you relax and believe in yourself, you will present yourself as the best candidate for the job. With persistence and determination, and a little practice, almost anyone can learn to interview with confidence and composure.

Come up with a general idea of how you might answer the common questions asked in virtually all interviews. Practice your answers but don't memorize them. Don't be afraid to take a minute before answering to gather your thoughts. A well thought out answer is better than one off the cuff.

Take the time, a day or two before the interview, to mentally review your accomplishments and the high points of your résumé. You should be able to rattle off your qualifications, your academic credentials, and your successful career experiences as effortlessly as reciting your name and phone number.

There are literally hundreds of interview questions that can be asked in an interview. It's impossible and unrealistic to attempt to practice answers to all of them. If you get caught up in memorizing answers to questions, you will be doing yourself a disservice. Memorized answers sound canned and unnatural.

COMMON INTERVIEW QUESTIONS

The following is a list of some of the most frequently asked interview questions. Study up!

- What are your strengths?
- Tell me about your last positions. Which ones have you enjoyed the most? Least?
- Are you willing to travel or relocate?
- Are you happy with your career progress to date?
- What are your career goals?
- Tell me about yourself.
- Where do you see yourself five years from now?
- What do you expect to get out of your career?
- What makes a sales representative successful?
- What is the most difficult situation that you have ever faced?
- How do you define success?
- What were the three most important events (positive or negative) in your life?
- What is your most significant accomplishment?
- What is your favorite book?
- What do you like and dislike about presentations and why?
- Tell me about your last day at work.
- What are the things that motivate you?
- What is the most difficult situation that you have ever faced?
- If money was no object, and you wanted to work, what would be your ideal position?
- What are your foreign language capabilities?
- What jobs have you enjoyed the most and the least and why?
- What actions would you take if we hired you?
- What can you offer us that someone else can't?
- Tell me about your education. Do you have plans for further education?
- What makes a good leader? Do you consider yourself to be a leader?
- Why do you want to leave your present employer?
- How has your schooling prepared you for this job?
- How would your current supervisor describe you?
- What are your primary activities outside of work?

- How do you handle people that you don't get along with?
- What makes you think you can handle this position?
- With what other companies are you interviewing?
- What has been your greatest challenge?
- What do you look for in a job?
- How long will it take for you to make a meaningful contribution to this company?
- How would this assignment fit your overall career plan?
- What three adjectives would you say best describe you?

> A Pfizer manager asked one of my customers to **"Define integrity."**
>
> The same manager also asked: *"Do you work better as an individual or as a team?"*
>
> My customer answered with: *"I work well as an individual or as a part of a team."*
>
> The manager replied with: *"Choose one."*
>
> My customer answered with: *"As an individual."*
>
> The manager replied with: *"We work in teams here."*

Questions Asked of Recent College Graduates:
- What is your GPA? Do you feel it reflects your abilities?
- How has your educational experience prepared you for this position?
- What was your favorite course in college and why?
- Why did you decide to attend X College? Are you happy with your choice?
- What factors did you consider in choosing your major?
- How did your college experience change you?

Common Interview Questions Revisited:
Tips for some of the tricky ones

- **Tell me about yourself.** *You must be able to answer this one. It's a definite!*
  Managers may be looking for various answers but the bottom line is that they want to know if you have what it takes to succeed in pharmaceutical sales. They want to see what type of person you are and they are looking for personality with this answer.

The best way to begin to answer is to ask them where they would like you to begin. If they are interested only in your time with your current employer, why start out talking about college?

Once you find out where to begin, make a short, organized statement of your achievements, and goals. You know from reading this book what qualifications managers are looking for. Give a brief overview of your résumé. As you talk about your skills, and achievements, relay their relevance to a successful pharmaceutical sales career.

• Why did you leave your last position?

The interviewer may want to know if you had any problems in your last job. If you didn't, simply give the reason for leaving and focus on your goals for yourself and your career. If you did, never describe that employer in negative terms. Try to avoid too many details and explain that you have set new goals for yourself and your career. An example may be "I've set some new goals for myself and my career. I have decided to follow my goals and explore new options. My goal is to continue to advance myself and excel in pharmaceutical sales."

• What is your major weakness?

Be positive: Turn a weakness into a strength. For example, you might say, "I'm a perfectionist. Sometimes I focus too much on making sure the job is done right."

• What are your salary expectations?

Postpone the salary discussion until you have all the facts. You need as much information as possible before making a decision. You might say, "I really need more information about the job before I can say. Maybe you can tell me about what you have budgeted and how your commission structure works." Follow up with any unanswered questions about the job that you may need answered.

• Why do you want to work here?

This is a very important question so it is important to answer with clarity and enthusiasm. Show that you have done your homework and that you have learned about the industry, the company and the job. Talk about your personality traits and mention that you feel that you are well suited for pharmaceutical sales. Talk about your skills and how you can benefit the company.

- **What special aspects of your professional experience have prepared you for this job?**

  Now is **not** the time to be modest. It's time to brag and convince the manager that you are the best one for the job! Focus on sales skills, anatomy and physiology knowledge, public speaking skills, leadership positions, teamwork, etc. This question is similar to the "tell me about yourself" question. Answer in a similar fashion, referring to your résumé for backup.

- **Can you describe for me one or two of your most important accomplishments?**

  Only you can answer this. Look into your past and be honest. What are you most proud of? The interviewer wants to know about you. They want to see you smile as you talk about your accomplishments. You should also talk about the future accomplishments you hope to make as you pursue a pharmaceutical sales career. The best accomplishments are yet to come!

- **What is the biggest obstacle that you have had to face in your current job or in your career?**

  The interviewer wants to know that you can face an obstacle and overcome it. Give some background information about an obstacle that you have faced and talk him/her through your thought process for overcoming the obstacle.

  Keep in mind that as a pharmaceutical rep, you will deal with obstacles on a daily basis. A gatekeeper at the front desk is just one obstacle that you may encounter.

  Sample Answer: *"I really wanted to become a pharmaceutical sales rep and I began my search three years ago. However, I realized with the high level of competition in the industry, that an associate's degree was not enough to go up against the competition. With this in mind, and a great desire to break into this industry, I opted to temporarily pursue a career in sales where I could prove myself and also attend school to complete my bachelor's degree. Now I am back to fully overcome the obstacle!"*

PHARMACEUTICAL SALES SPECIFIC INTERVIEW QUESTIONS:

- **What types of things did you do to outsell your competition?**

  The manager wants to know what your sales style is. Focus on your creativity and hard work. Specify instances where you studied harder, worked harder, and built quality relationships. Tell a story about how your efforts paid off and tell it with a lot of pride and enthusiasm.

- **Why do you want to become a pharmaceutical sales representative?**

  You will definitely hear this question!

The interviewer is seeking an answer that conveys your love of selling and your desire to sell pharmaceuticals specifically. This is a great opportunity to inform the interviewer that you have researched the industry and that you have a good grasp of what it takes to be a pharmaceutical sales rep. Show him/her that you have a sincere desire to become a pharmaceutical sales rep, that you are well qualified, and can't wait to prove yourself.

Sample Answer: *"The more I research the pharmaceutical industry and this job, the more eager I am to become a pharmaceutical sales representative! Deep down, I know that pharmaceutical sales is the job for me! I love the fact that I would be learning about drugs and would have the opportunity to sell to professionals and their office staff. It would be an ideal fit for my personality and my talents. I have found that the ability to persuade people comes naturally for me. I also know that success in pharmaceutical sales is based on building relationships. I was a master at building relationships in my previous job and I can't wait to show my talents in pharmaceutical sales."*

- **You don't have any experience in sales. How do you plan on learning what you need to know to be successful in selling?**

  Without sales experience, it is essential you convince the interviewer that you have an understanding of the sales process. Demonstrate to the interviewer that you have what it takes to make it in sales (communication skills, leadership skills, and rapport building skills). Explain that all you need is the opportunity to prove yourself and given the chance, you know you will excel. Tell the interviewer you know sales are based not only on the ability of persuasion but also on gaining trust and building rapport. You may want to give an example of a time that you were able to persuade someone or perhaps cite the fact that you are great at building and maintaining relationships with customers.

  Sample Answer: *"Although I do not have sales experience, I am quick to learn new tasks and have a good understanding of what it takes to be successful when selling pharmaceuticals. I have the personality to sell successfully and the ability to build long lasting relationships with office staff and physicians. I am personable, enthusiastic and creative. Those innate personality traits are really what it takes to make it in sales. I have those traits and cannot wait to show you what I am capable of."*

- **What do you think it takes to be successful in selling?**

  There are many ways to be successful in selling but all sales reps in pharmaceutical sales must possess the following to excel: They must be able to differentiate themselves from the competition, must have the drive and dedication to see the docs, and get their message across. They must also have a strong belief in their product. If there is no enthusiasm for what they are doing and selling, it will show through in their sales presentations and ultimately will affect sales.

Sample Answer: *"With so many representatives in this industry, I believe the biggest challenge is to differentiate yourself and your products from the competition. By differentiating yourself from the competition, you will probably get more time with the physician. More time with a physician means more time to talk about your product and more time to increase sales."* (Give examples of how you have differentiated yourself or been very creative.)

- **How do you handle rejection?**

Pharmaceutical reps are faced with rejection on a daily basis. The interviewer will want to be assured that you can persevere when faced with rejection. Give an example of when you were faced with rejection and explain how you handled the rejection.

Sample Answer: *"I realize that rejection is a part of sales and I do not take rejection personally. In my current position, I deal with rejection frequently. I analyze every situation and try to grow from it. I try to figure out why they rejected my offer and come up with a new plan for my next visit. In my opinion, rejection is an opportunity to sell. If every call was easy and every person on every call was willing to give me 100% of their business, that would take the fun and the challenge out of selling. I thrive on overcoming rejection and ultimately, making the sale."*

- **How do you plan to increase sales? How long do you estimate that it will take you to make an impact on sales in your territory?**

The manager wants to know that you have a specific plan to increase sales and that you have an idea of what it takes to make it in this business. You will need to answer in a way that shows your motivation and dedication to increasing sales.

Sample Answer: *"Initially, my goal would be to excel in sales training and product knowledge. Being well-prepared and knowledgeable out of the gate is a great start. From there, I would get organized and learn my territory and my business. I will use sales data to find potential and focus on my customers with the most potential. Once I locate them, I will do everything possible to find out what makes them tick. I want to know why they prescribe what they prescribe. If they won't see me, I will work every avenue to see them. I will try them before office hours, after office hours, at the hospital, whatever it takes. I know that the best way to increase sales is to get the message to the doctors and to remind them as often as possible."*

"I realize that building a territory takes time. Relationships need to be built. I'm not looking to increase sales in an unrealistic amount of time. I am here for the long run. I know that doctors don't change their prescribing habits overnight. I think that the key to increasing sales is being well-prepared, working hard at seeing my customers and getting to know them and their prescribing habits over time. Once I can gain their trust, I can gain their commitment. Increasing sales doesn't just happen-it takes time, a great plan of action, and dedication. Eventually hard work pays off."

• **Sell me this pen** (*or other object in a role play scenario*).

PLEASE NOTE: If you make it to the final interviews, you can bet that you will be asked to role-play. You will need to know the basics of the sales call. Usually the interviewer poses as the doctor and you are the rep selling to the doctor. **Practice this one!**

This is a task that is dreaded by many, especially those with limited or no sales experience. For those with sales experience, however, it is a simple task. By following a basic sales call formula, anyone can learn to sell any object. The key is to be familiar with the basic components of the sales call (basic is just fine for interview purposes.)

Anatomy of a simple sales call:

1. **Introduce yourself, your company, and your company name.**

For example: *"Hello Doctor Smith, it's nice to see you again. I'm Lauren Lane your Pharmacia rep. Today I would like to tell you about a new product that I think you are going to like a lot. Can I have a few minutes with you to tell you about this pen?"*
Show them the pen but don't let them handle it.

2. **Uncover your customer's needs.**

What are they looking for in a pen? Do they want one that writes longer than any other pen or are they looking for a Mont Blanc-type of pen that portrays a successful, professional image?

Discover the customer's needs and you will know what features of the pen to emphasize. If you want to talk about the great felt tip and the customer could care less about the felt tip, don't focus your sales call on the felt tip. If you do, you will not sell any pens!

How do you uncover your customer's needs? You ask them!

For example: *"Doctor, before I begin to tell you about this pen, I would like to find out about the pens that you currently use. I know that there are other pens that you use and like. What is it that makes you choose one pen over another?"* Use an open-ended question.

3. **Listen.**

Listen to what the customer tells you because they are telling you what their needs are. For example, a customer might say, "I like a pen that has a nice grip and the ink color is really important to me."

4. **Use feature and benefit selling to show them that your product meets their needs.**

You have uncovered their needs and you know what they are looking for in a pen: Show them via very basic feature and benefit selling that your pen is one that they will like and should use.

What is a feature?

A feature is a physical component of the pen. Examples of features of the pen:

- Felt tip
- Black ink
- Comfortable grip
- Size
- Overall look

What is a benefit?

A benefit is always a benefit of a particular feature and answers the question, "So what?"

For example: *"This pen has a quick dry tip"* (feature). *"Because it has a quick dry tip, you can rest assured that all of the prescriptions that you write will be smudge proof, eliminating calls from pharmacists who can't make out your writing"* (benefit).

The interviewer may mention more than one need. Cover all of them with feature and benefit selling.

5. **Close**

Once you have demonstrated that your pen meets all of the interviewer's needs, ask him/her a question which will give the interviewer an opportunity to give you an objection if there is one. If there's no objection, you will close and ask for the business.

For example: *"Doctor, you said that you are interested in a pen that is smudge proof and has a nice grip. Have I shown you that this pen is smudge proof and has a nice grip?"*

If the interviewer has an objection, listen to it and address the issue. If there is no objection, close!

For example: *"Doctor, it sounds to me like this pen is one that you can really put to good use. Would you agree? Would you be willing to give this pen a try?"*

When the doctor agrees to try the pen. Thank them and tell them that you are looking forward to coming back and getting their feedback.

The following five questions are from PharmaceuticalInterviewQuestions.com.

- **What is your perception of a typical day for a pharmaceutical sales rep?**

Thought Process: The hiring manager is looking for your perception of what the representative does every day. They are also looking for work ethic (working early, late) and commitment to getting the job done. The more you can parallel what you are currently doing to the pharmaceutical representative's day, the better off you are. Show them you have done research and have spoken with someone in the industry.

Note: If you can ride with a representative do so.

Sample Answer: *"I have an idea of what the day is like for a pharmaceutical representative and I think it parallels some of what my normal day is like. As a representative I would see as many of my assigned physicians as possible and sell them on why they should use my drug over the competition. I know some physicians are difficult to reach, so I would try to catch them early (6–7a.m.) in the hospital or after hours, like I have to do with some of my customers. Some days I would utilize a lunch to better impact difficult-to-see physicians. After 5 p.m., I would enter my calls in the computer (or after each call) and pick up e-mails. At night I would look over pre-call planning for my next day. I don't know if you entertain physicians like I do with my customers currently but I would do some entertaining at night (restaurant) or on weekends — (golf, hunting, fishing) — whatever it takes to make my numbers."*

- **What do you think is the most challenging aspect of a pharmaceutical representative's job?**

  Thought Process: Again, the hiring manager wants to determine if you know the true challenges a representative faces daily and if you have the skills to meet these challenges.

  Sample Answer:*"I think it's probably getting quality time with the physician to impact prescribing behavior. Another challenge I think you would face is there are physicians who don't see representatives. You have to be creative in finding a way to gain access to them."*

- **You are given a territory and a list of physicians to call on. How would you organize and prioritize your call schedule?**

  Thought Process: The hiring manager wants to feel confident that you set your priorities based on the greatest return on time invested. You should organize your territory based on calling on the customers with the greatest sales potential. The manager is looking to see if you know the "80/20"rule. (80% of your business comes from 20% of your customers. Your goal is to find the 20% as quickly as you can. After the 20% have been contacted, you move down the list and work on developing new clients).

  Sample Answer: "I would analyze my territory, and determine the accounts that have the greatest sales potential. I would quickly work to determine my most profitable 20% of my clients. Once they have been contacted and I feel comfortable with my relationship with these clients, I would then work the rest of my customers and develop new clients.

- **Tell me about your last manager. Did you like him/her? If I was your manager, what is the best way to coach/mentor you to success? What qualities should a successful manager possess? Describe the relationship that should exist between the supervisor and those reporting to him or her.**

Thought Process: The hiring manger wants to know if he/she can work with you. The hiring manager is also looking at your perception of authority, your willingness to learn, how you handle criticism, and how you like to be managed. The hiring manager needs to know how to manage each of his/her sales representatives and provide the support and or tools to help the sales representative meet the goals. The relationship that should exist between the manager and sales representative should be open, honest, encouraging, and accountable on both sides. Be careful on how you answer this question. Again, no former manager bashing allowed!

Sample Answer: *"I liked my manager and we had a positive working relationship. We had similar thought processes on how to run my territory and how to best manage me. The best way to manage me is to give me all the tools (training, funding) necessary to be successful. Then let me run my territory in a way to exceed expectations. I would like a manager who periodically rides with me so he/she can understand my account and provide open constructive criticism. I view my territory as my own business and take accountability for its performance. I feel the successful qualities in a manager includes: high expectations, openness, honesty, excellent communication skills and the ability to assist me in my career development and goal attainment. I want an open and candid relationship with my manager."*

- **How do you think you would get a physician to switch to your drug?**

Thought Process: The hiring manger is looking for sales skills and your strategic process in dealing with physicians.

Sample Answer: *"First, I would NOT expect the physician to make a sudden change to my drug if he or she is happy with the drug they're currently prescribing. I am going to have to start small and expand the doctor's usage by nibbling away at market share. I would determine what influences the doctor's behavior — reprints, speaker programs, peers, and formularies. I would use a combination of the appropriate tools to gain the physician's agreement on my drug's effectiveness. After this, I would gain commitment from the doctor to use the drug on a specific patient type. After the physician has tried my drug on this patient type, I would get the doctor to notice the success on this patient when the patient comes back in for a follow up visit. When the physician admitted efficacy, I would then gain commitment for use in other patient types. This is comparable with my current business."*

THE DREADED (BUT NOT SO BAD) SITUATIONAL QUESTIONS:

Situational questions are usually asked at some point in the pharmaceutical sales interview process. These questions are usually hypothetical in nature and are asked to see how you would react if you were in a similar situation. Managers like to ask these questions to find out a bit more about your character and personality.

> **Steve, who was interviewing with AstraZeneca, offered the following:**
> "With AstraZeneca, they really emphasize the situational type questions in the interview and you have to answer them in the 'STAR' format. The 'STAR' questions took up about half of the time in the interviews that I had with the company. They are not difficult, but you must think quickly, be clear, not too verbose, and stick to the format. A question that I was asked was, *'Give an example of a time when you did something at work that your boss didn't like even though you thought that you had done a good job on it and explain what happened.'*"

Your interviewer may or may not request that you answer in the 'STAR' format. Regardless of what they request, 'STAR' is always a good answer format to use, particularly when answering situational questions.

S=Situation   (Reiterate the **situation** that you were in)
T=Task   (Tell about the **task** that you needed to complete)
A=Action   (Talk about the **action** that you took)
R=Result   (Tell about the results of your actions)

> **Carla, who interviewed with Innovex, offered the following:**
> "My phone interview was with a person from an outside company who was hired to do the phone screening. The woman sounded like she had just interviewed about 100 people. She was very matter of fact and to the point…almost like she couldn't wait for the day to end. Needless to say, it was tough to get a conversation going with her. She told me I had 20 minutes to answer six situational questions and that she would be taking notes by hand. I was asked: *'What would you do if you encountered a doctor who was annoyed that you were in his office because your counterpart was just in 10 minutes ago promoting the same products?'* "

There are literally thousands of situational questions that can be asked and there are no right or wrong answers. Since studying the 'correct' answers is literally impossible, your best bet is to think about the question that is being asked and answer with sincerity and clarity.

Situational Questions:

• **How will you get to see a doctor who is very difficult to see?**
The manager wants to know that you will not settle with seeing only those docs who are easy to see. They are looking for your creative and persistent side.

Sample Answer: *"I realize that physicians are getting more and more difficult to see simply because the number of reps calling on them has increased dramatically over the years. I think that the key to seeing these difficult to see doctors is to "think outside of the box" so to speak. First I need to analyze the situation. Is the doctor difficult to see, or is the receptionist making it difficult for me to see the doctor? If the doctor is difficult to see, I need to really work on that receptionist to get her or him to open up to me. The receptionist may have some great information that will help me get in to see the doctor and by getting to know the receptionist and getting on her or his good side, I should be able to get some good information and come up with a plan. Maybe the receptionist can tell me when the doctor's birthday is. Showing up with a cake on the doctor's birthday may be what it takes to make it in the door. Perhaps it's just a matter of getting there at a particular time of day. Before or after office hours may be best or even at the hospital. Every situation and person is different. Good sales people learn how to uncover opportunities by working smart. It just takes a little creative thinking and acting on it."*

- **What would you do if a doctor asked you a question that you couldn't answer?**

Sample Answer: *"I would acknowledge that I didn't know the answer and try, initially, to find an answer while still in the doctor's office. Perhaps just referring to the product's package insert would help me out, or I might have the answer with me in my documentation. If I couldn't find the answer while there, I would make it a priority to find the answer and get back to the doctor within 24 hours. Coming back the next day with an answer to the question would actually be a great excuse for a follow up call. The last thing that I would want to do would be to attempt to answer a question that I didn't know the answer to. I'm building a relationship in that office and have a reputation to rely on. I don't want to ruin my credibility by answering incorrectly. I think that it is reasonable to believe that our customers don't expect us to know everything and they respect us when we admit that we can't answer correctly at that given moment."*

- **This job requires that you co-promote one of our products with an employee from another one of our divisions. As a team, you will be required to increase sales of a particular product in this territory. Suppose that you get this job and you find that you are getting little or no help from your counterpart. How would you handle this situation?**

The manager wants to be sure that you are able to work well as a part of a team and to see how you would handle a situation that can negatively impact your sales.

Sample Answer: *"I know that co-promoting products is often a part of the pharmaceutical sales job nowadays. A good working relationship with a counterpart is always key to motivating each other and ultimately, driving sales. Assuming that I had a good working relationship with my counterpart, I would arrange to meet for breakfast before we headed out to our territories for the day. During breakfast, I would try to uncover the problem. Perhaps just a bit of help from me can really help them come around. Maybe they need just a little more help with their product knowledge. They may be new in the territory and might need some extra help getting in to see their key doctors. There are a whole host of reasons why this person may not be performing to their full potential. A good teammate should always be there to help the other one. Maximum effort by two people in a territory is always better than just one. If I have the help of another fully capable person in my territory, it will be my goal to help them help me."*

- **What would you do if one of your doctors kept telling you that he or she was writing prescriptions for your product when the doctor really wasn't?**

Suggestion: It is best to figure out a solution to the problem without being confrontational. Remember that this could be one of your high volume prescribers and you need him or her to help drive your business. If you confront the doctor on the issue, you risk being banned from the office.

Sample Answer: *"My guess is that if a doctor is lying, it's probably because he or she doesn't want to give me an objection. Maybe it's just easier for the doctor to agree and tell me that he or she is using the drug. Bottom line is that the doctor still has an objection and I need to uncover the objection and overcome it. I would thank the doctor for the business and might also mention the names of a couple of his peers who are using the product and give the doctor some specific feedback about the results that they are getting with the product. Indirectly, I would still try to sell the product. I might say, 'I know that you are not using my product **all** of the time and on every patient, so I would like you to consider expanding your usage.' I might then give the doctor examples of patient types that he or she should consider trying it on. Next, I would ask what product the doctor currently uses for that patient type and why. After finding out why the doctor is using a competing product, I would explain how my product is superior to that one and ask the doctor if he would consider using my product instead of another product when that patient type comes along."*

Feedback from interviewees who have survived pharma sales job interviews.

(When you read this, remember that interview formats and expectations are always changing)

PFIZER:
- Managers like to see brag books and often will ask if they can keep a copy.
- Hire outstanding recent grads.
- Often hire teachers.
- Phone interview is often conducted by an outside company who will take notes during the interview and who will invite you back for a face to face with the manager or managers if all goes well.
- Often ask: "What do you know about the Pharmaceutical Industry?"
- Be ready at least 30 minutes early for your phone interview.....they may call you early to catch you off guard!

MERCK:
- Outside company tends to do phone screens. Scheduled to last a half hour.
- Interviewer can be standoffish and tough to get a conversation going. Also expect a considerable pause between questions as they take notes during the interview.
- If the candidate passes the phone screen, a Merck rep will contact the candidate.
- Tend to like to ask behavioral questions.
- Some questions that they like to ask are:
    1. "Describe the first time that you had to work your hardest to communicate information to someone at work. What was the outcome?"
    2. Another is: "Tell me about a situation where you had to influence other members of a team to implement a course of action and what were the results."
    3. "When did you have to review company policy in regard to making a decision and what did you do?"
    4. "Tell me about a time when you had to adjust your priorities to achieve a goal."
    5. "What do you know about Merck?"

- Some key actions that Merck is looking for:
    1. Demonstrates appropriate use of interpersonal styles and communication methods to gain acceptance of ideas.
    2. Articulate, expresses oneself clearly.
    3. Characterized by self-control and self-assurance.
    4. Actively acknowledges what was said in a conversation. Seeks clarification and checks for understanding.

BRISTOL-MEYERS SQUIBB COMPANY:
- Have been known to ask, "Why are you going to excel in pharmaceutical sales?"
- Also: "How do you learn technical information?"

ELI LILLY AND COMPANY:
- Have asked: "Give me an example of your best sale."

ORGANON:
- For second interview, they have asked their candidates to present plans to creatively impact the market with 3 of their drugs.
- First 6 months goals.
- Career goals.

BOEHRINGER INGELHEIM CORP:
- Questions that they have asked include:
  1. "What do you think a typical day is like for a pharmaceutical representative?"
  2. "What do you know about Boehringer Ingelheim?"
  3. "What is the organization like where you currently work?"
  4. "How many hours per day and week did you work?"
  5. "How did you get your leads?"
  6. "Have you ever gone on a sales call with a pharmaceutical rep?"
  7. "What daily priorities did you set to accomplish tasks?"
  8. "What was your average business sale in dollars?"
- Chosen candidates will be expected to score at least an 80% on tests while in training.
- Training consists of two-3 week classes. Initially, there is also a 3 week home study as well.

CRUCIAL CLOSING QUESTIONS THAT YOU SHOULD ASK YOUR INTERVIEWER:

Asking these questions will help you advance to the next step in the interview process.

1. What additional information do you need regarding my candidacy?
2. Can you please explain the rest of the interview process? Where do I go from here?
3. Is there anything that is preventing me from continuing on in the interview process?
4. How do I compare to my competition?
5. Can we set up the next interview now?

BRAGBOOKS:
WHAT IS A BRAG BOOK AND HOW DO I MAKE ONE?

What is a bragbook?

A brag book is a must have for any face-to-face pharmaceutical sales interview. If you want to stand out from the competition and add credibility to the claims that you make in your résumé, you should spend a little time putting a bragbook together.

The bragbook is a sales aid and no true salesperson should interview without one. Just as salespeople rely on a sales aid to sell the features and benefits of their service or product, you should have a bragbook to sell yourself to your interviewer.

What is the purpose of a bragbook?

A bragbook, if well-constructed and used properly in an interview, can add life and credibility to your résumé. It can also help your interviewer remember more details about you when the interview day is done.

What do I include in my bragbook?

Take a look at your résumé. Make a list of all of your accomplishments and then think about how you can document them in your bragbook. You want to include tangible evidence of as many achievements as possible. For some, this may be an easy task. For those of us who tend not to save everything, it may take some digging and may also require a few phone calls to get some of this information in writing.

Some ideas of what to include

- Notes from company personnel congratulating you on your most recent sales award.
- If you have a wall plaque that documents your sales achievements, make a copy of the front of it and include it.
- Performance reviews.
- Ranking reports that show your performance.
- Recent college grads can include college transcript with GPA, if a 3.0 or better.

- Letters of recommendation from previous employers, professors, etc.
- Certificates of completion of any special courses that you have taken.
- Photos of you accepting awards.
- Pay stub that shows your outstanding commissions with previous employer.
- Documented achievements that show your leadership skills or positions held.
- Business card that shows your previous job title.
- President's club status notification.
- Photos of yourself at the president's club trip.

Creative tips to help your bragbook stand out:

Do you want to go into an interview with a bragbook that WOWS your interviewer? The following are some creative ideas that really helped candidates stand out in some of the interviews that I conducted.

(Suggestion: Remember that your bragbook is a reflection of you. Choose to add only the material that you think will fit your personality.)

1. One candidate had his kids create a page for his bragbook. They drew a picture of their dad and wrote some adjectives to describe him.

(*I liked this a lot because it really helped me see him as a creative person who also liked to be around his kids. It also brought up great conversation and got a lot of smiles! I will warn you, however that this idea can also open up a can of worms. Even though your interviewer shouldn't be asking about your family and plans for a family, this can entice them to broach the subject. They may also make assumptions based on the fact that you have children. If you don't want to go down that path, don't include this page.)*

2. One woman included a photo of herself competing in a triathlon.

(*I liked this addition to the bragbook because it made her into a "person". She was not just a person with numbers to show me. I really like when a candidate can add personality to their interview....this touch certainly did just that. By adding her photo, it also helped me to better remember her.)*

3. A recent grad added her graduation photo to the cover of her brag-book. The cover said, "This motivated graduate will make a great addition to sales team. Here's why:"

(*I also liked this idea but I would warn that if you try this, you will want to make sure that it still looks professional. In other words, don't do this and handwrite the text. Her cover looked impressive yet still professional.)

4. Create a 90 day plan of action. This idea was emailed to me by one of my customers and for obvious reasons, I liked it a lot! Here is her idea:

Lisa –

I cannot begin to tell you how much of a help your book has been to me. I just nailed my second interview with Pfizer after taking every bit of advice from you book. I felt like I had an edge over all of my competition!!

.......I put together a brag book, which the district manager actually asked me, "What else do you have in there?!"

Something that really impressed the district manager today was my "90 Day Plan of Action." I put together a list of 10 goals I would like to complete within my first 90 days of employment at Pfizer. I think things like this set me apart from my competition.

Karie D.

Illinois

**Karie's
90 DAY PLAN OF ACTION**

GOAL 1:
Successfully complete Pfizer training. EXCEED expectations.

GOAL 2:
Become familiar with established territory and meet
with partners and managers.

GOAL 3:
Research the status of my territory.

GOAL 4:
Understand the local status of my products in hospitals
and doctor's offices.

GOAL 5:
Understand and become familiar with the status of the formulary.

GOAL 6:
Know who my major customers are:
Who are those 20% who will give me 80% of my business?

GOAL 7:
Research my competition and my competing products.

GOAL 8:
Work with my counterparts. Join them on meetings and calls.

GOAL 9:
Develop a strategic plan of action for my daily sales calls
and set goals.

GOAL 10:
Act on my training and become a blockbuster sales representative!

---

5. Show them on a separate page that you are the ideal candidate and the
   one for the job. Here's how:

Create a page that lists skills/attributes of the ideal sales representative on the left side of the page. On the right side of the page, show how you meet or exceed their expectations.

Some skills that you may want to list might include:
- Meets/exceeds sales goals
- Team Player
- Dependable
- Self Motivated
- Good public speaker
- Outgoing/Excellent communicator
- Creative
- Grasps new ideas/challenges with ease
- Leadership skills
- Organized
- Good listener
- Enthusiastic
- Hard worker

How do I assemble my bragbook?

After collecting your documentation, take note of how many pages you have. Go to a local office supply store and purchase a sales binder with clear plastic insert pages (a.k.a. a pitch book). Pitch books are sold with varying numbers of pages so choose the size that will best accommodate your needs. Before putting your pages into the book, highlight the main points on each page in yellow marker. Assemble it in reverse chronological order with your most recent documentation first. You may want to tab your pages for quick accesses if you have a lot of information.

How do I use my bragbook?

When a question comes up about your accomplishments and/or achievements, answer the question and then refer to the sections of the bragbook that back up your claims. Use a pencil and refer to the highlighted points (you don't want the interviewer to have to read all of the information).

Practice using your bragbook and remember where your information is located within the pages. The last thing that you want to do is fumble around for the information. Also, keep in mind that it is not necessary to show all your information. Play it by ear and if the interviewer is truly interested in seeing it all, by all means, brag away! If the interviewer seems uninterested, don't continually refer to your book. The bragbook is meant to support and back up your verbal answers to questions. Don't rely on it to answer your questions.

Ideas of what to include in my bragbook:

1.

2.

3.

4.

5.

6.

7.

8.

9.

10.

Section 6:
Pharmaceutical Sales Job Fairs and Working with Recruiters

▷ ▷ ▷

PHARMACEUTICAL SALES JOB FAIRS: TO ATTEND OR NOT TO ATTEND...THAT IS THE QUESTION!

Someone who recently returned from a pharmaceutical sales job fair told me that I should also consider selling T-shirts on my website. He even suggested a slogan:

"I went to a pharmaceutical sales job fair and all I got was this lousy tee shirt!"

Is that enough said about pharmaceutical job fairs? My opinion is NO!

Regardless of your experience when you get there, pharmaceutical sales job-fairs are well-worth attending. If you don't land a job as a result of attending one, just the fact that you have attended is a great learning experience. Keep in mind that every job fair is different. Just because you have been to one and had no luck doesn't mean that you should write them off.

Keep going and keep networking!

The following are some websites who specialize in sales career fairs or who have been known to have pharmaceutical companies in attendance. Visit their sites for a career fair schedule.

www.salestrax.com
www.hirequest.com
www.jobexpo.com
www.careersummit.com
www.bessiresales.com
www.diversitycareergroup.com

How to make the most of your time on the job fair floor to beat your competitors:

• Find out which companies will be attending the fair and be prepared to answer the question, "Why do you want to work for us?" (Refer to *www.hoovers.com* and *www.bloomberg.com* to research the companies.)

- Plan to take at least 25 copies of your résumé to a job fair. The scannable format is probably best for job fairs because it accommodates most of the ways employers file and distribute paper résumés and their electronic counterparts. Bring a pen, pencil and notepad too, and organize it all in a nice brief case or portfolio.

- Come prepared to interview on the spot. You will more than likely interview summary style in a few minutes or less. In other words, be prepared to quickly sell your skills, talents and experiences. Job fairs tend to be more casual than formal interviews, so you can relax and be more friendly. But also "read the mood" of the employer's representative with whom you're speaking at the moment, and adjust your style accordingly. Even though it's more casual, attire, body language, and professionalism still count. Dress sharp, act professional and most importantly smile and be enthusiastic.

- Prepare to fill out a job application on the spot. Unless you are told otherwise, it's best to turn it in right away. Taking it home first allows your competitors to beat you to it.

- Arrive a few minutes early at a job fair, to register if required and plan your "attack." Pick up a booth map if available, and route your path to the employers that you would like to visit.

- Visit your targeted employers first with résumé in hand, and spend some "quality time" with each of them.

- When wrapping up your conversations with employers' reps, show your interest by asking them what the next steps are. Ask if it's okay to call them or send follow-up letters a few days after the job fair ends.

- Keep track of which companies you talk to and jot down other notes right after you speak with their rep. Collect business cards or contact info as you go, and follow up within 24–48 hours.

PHARMACEUTICAL ASSOCIATIONS: A GREAT PLACE TO NETWORK!

If you have a pharmaceutical association in your area, consider yourself lucky: It can be a great networking resource! Contact the president of the association in your area for information about upcoming meetings and ask if you can attend. Most of their meetings are very informal and are usually social get-togethers for reps to exchange ideas and check in on the competition. If you can attend a meeting, take your résumé and do some networking!

*The association information listed below is as current and complete as possible. This is not a comprehensive list.

■ *ALASKA:*

Alaska Pharmaceutical Representative Association
P.O. Box 771753
Eagle River, AK 99577-1753
Phone: (907) 689-7736
Alternate Phone: Fax: (907) 689-7802
Steve Harris, president
Email: *alaskapharmaceuticalreps@hotmail.com*

■ *CALIFORNIA:*

Pharmaceutical Representatives of Stanislaus County
Phone: (209) 669-8301
Alternate Phone: (209) 869-2019
Mike Isola
Curtis Lineberger

SCPC (South Coast Pharmaceutical Committee, HIV specialists)
Orange Co., Long Beach and Palm Springs
Phone: (949) 770-4489
Kimberly Murdock
Email: *kimberly.murdock@abbott.com*

■ *FLORIDA:*

SFPPA (South Florida Professional Pharmaceutical Association)
Miami-Dade, Broward, Palm Beach counties
www.sfppa.org
Email: *info@sfppa.org*

Volusia County Pharmaceutical Representative Association
Julie McGuire, president
Email: *VCPRA@aol.com*

■ *GEORGIA:*

Atlanta Medical & Pharmaceutical Representatives' Association
Phone: (404) 525-2110
Ray Thatch, president
Reno Odish, treasurer
www.ampra.com

National Association of Professional Pharmaceutical Representatives of Atlanta
P.O. Box 161902
Atlanta, GA 30321
Phone: (770) 621-5746
Jamal Grooms, president

■ *ILLINOIS:*

Illini Pharmaceutical Representatives Association (IPPRA)
David Lee
www.ippra.org
Email: *webmaster@ippra.org*

NIMRA (Northern Illinois Medical Representative Association – Rockford)
Phone: (815) 227-4502
Todd Warda, president

■ *INDIANA:*

Indiana Medical and Pharmaceutical Representative Association
10229 Lower Huntington Road
Roanoke, IN 46783
Phone: (260) 409-2610
Jack Young
Email: *championwithin@aol.com*

■ *KANSAS:*

Topeka Pharmaceutical Representatives' Association
2787 SW Plass St.
Topeka, KS 66111
Tava Weidenbaker, president
Email: *tavaweidenbaker@aol.com*

■ *KENTUCKY:*

Greater Louisville Pharmaceutical Representative Association
Phone: (800) 624-2542 ext. 2686
Frank S. Schramko
Email: *fschramk@ibius.jnj.com*

Professional Representative Organization of Northern Kentucky
Phone: (800) 656-5660 ext. 10491
Lance Derry, vice president
Jeff Overmann, treasurer
Email: *NKYPRO@yahoo.com*

■ *MICHIGAN:*

Western Michigan Pharmaceutical Representative Association
Phone: (616) 262-8861
Carolyn O'Grady
Email: *wmprs@yahoo.com*

Metro Detroit Pharmaceutical Representatives Assoc.
580 Thornhill Ct.
Belleville, MI 48111
Phone: (810) 287-1499
Shannon Ostby
Email: *sostby0427@aol.com*

Kalamazoo Area Pharmaceutical Rep Assoc. (KAPRA)
Margo Fitzgerald
Email: *kazookapra@yahoo.com*

Michigan Pharmaceutical Representative Society
815 N. Washington Ave.
Lansing, MI 48906
Phone: (517) 484-1466
Carmel Schwalm, chairwoman

PRIDE (Pharmaceutical Representatives in Detroit Excelling)
P.O. Box 4115
Southfield, MI 48037-4115
Phone: (248) 988-1061
Email: *pridepharm@yahoo.com*

■ *MINNESOTA:*

Twin Cities Pharmaceutical Representative Association
1360 University Ave W, #130
St. Paul, MN 55104
Phone: (651) 690-2485
www.tcpra.com

■ *ONTARIO:*

RAPTOR (Representative Association for Pharmaceuticals in Toronto)
7-16 Foxbar Rd,
Toronto, ON M4V 2G6
Canada
Shane Blanchard
Email: *blanch4@rogers.com*

■ *OREGON:*

Southern Oregon Pharmaceutical Representative Association
Phone: (541) 821-2391
Eugene Schulzke

■ *PENNSYLVANIA:*

Philadelphia Area Pharmaceutical Representative Association
Phone: (215) 801-5227
Jeff McGeary, president
Email: *phillyrepassn@aol.com*

■ *SOUTH CAROLINA:*

Medical Representatives of Columbia
Phone: (803) 356-6786
Ruth Ann Alexander

■ *TEXAS:*

Amarillo Pharmaceutical Representatives Assoc.
Amy Duncan, secretary
Email: *amy.duncan@spcorp.com*

LAMPS (Longview and Marshall Pharmaceutical Sales Reps)
Murry Hodge, president
Email: *murhodge@cox-internet.com*

Austin Pharmaceutical Representative Association
P.O. Box 696
Cedar Park, TX 78630
Phone: (800) 496-3772 ext. 87755
Stephen Blanton
Email: *stephen.blanton@astrazeneca.com*

■ *VIRGINIA:*

Pharmaceutical Representatives Assoc. of Southside Hampton Roads Inc. (PRASHR)
Extreme southeastern Virginia
Tom Cobin
www.prashr.org

■ *WISCONSIN:*

CWPRA (Central Wisconsin Pharmaceutical Representatives Association)
Phone: (877) 202-2721 ext. 4810
Alternate Phone: (866) 424-4260 ext. 8115130
Jay Hutchinson, president
Mike Noel, vice president
www.cwpra.com

WWPRA (Western Wisconsin Pharmaceutical Representative Association)
www.wwpra.com
Email: *wwpra@wwpra.com*

WORKING WITH PHARMACEUTICAL SALES RECRUITERS

The first two rules of thumb when working with a recruiter are to find a good one and to find one who specializes in pharmaceutical sales.

As a general rule, recruiters like to work with the most qualified candidates. They prefer to work with those with sales experience and a host of accomplishments and achievements. Why? Odds are very good that they will place that individual and when they place someone, they get paid. By choosing the cream of the crop, they save themselves time and make themselves money.

If a recent college grad tries to work with a recruiter to break into pharmaceutical sales, the grad will often be told to get other sales experience and then call back in a year or two. If you have limited experience, your best bet is to follow this step-by-step guide. If you have a great résumé and a lot to offer, the recruiter route is also a good way to go.

When you use a recruiter, the competition is greater than going directly through a rep referral. You will, however, have much less competition with a recruiter than you would if you applied to a national ad.

Recruiters normally select their top three candidates and send them directly to the district manager for interviews. If none of the three are selected for a second interview, the process begins again.

The best way to work with a recruiter:
Write, call, fax, or show up at their doorstep?

The most frequently asked question about working with recruiters is: Who Pays?

All executive search firms are paid by their corporate clients, not by individuals. No executive search firm should ever ask you for a fee for anything. If they do, they are not an executive search firm but an outplacement firm or employment agency.

If they ask for a fee from you, drop them like a hot potato! There are too many firms to choose from whose fees are paid by their clients. Don't waste your time and money on a company who wants to charge you a fee.

Most good search firms will also help you with interviewing skills, résumé writing, and letter writing, all for free! They want to help you get the job because they get paid when you get the offer.

The second most frequently asked question about working with recruiters is: What is the best way to contact them?

Hands down, mailing or emailing a cover letter and a résumé works best. Interested headhunters will call you. Don't bother calling them. They are great at blowing off calls and they definitely don't like knocks on their door!

RECRUITERS WHO SPECIALIZE IN PLACING PHARMACEUTICAL PROFESSIONALS

Before the Internet, I used to recommend using a local recruiter. Now recruiters are aware of openings all over the country. Don't limit yourself to your local recruiters.

Please note that this is not a comprehensive list. Some of the names and numbers may have changed since this printing.

Visit my website at *www.pharmaceuticalsalesinterviews.com* for targeted résumé distribution to over 150 pharm companies and recruiters.

Appleone
Phone: 1.800.564.5644
www.appleone.com

Fortune Personnel Consultants
Internet: *http://www.fpcweb.com*

Management Recruiters International
Internet: *http://www.brilliantpeople.com*
Multiple locations nationwide,

Tuler and Roth
Phone: 813.994.6524
Email: *info@tylerandroth.com*
Internet: *http://www.tylerandroth.com*

Snelling
Phone: 1.877.SNELLING
Internet: *http://www.snelling.com*
Multiple locations nationwide.
  See web site.

Southwestern Professional Services
Internet: *http://www.careerhunter.com*
        http://www.thinkingahead.com

Alabama

Healthcare Recruiters of Alabama
1945 Hoover Court
Suite 205
Birmingham, AL 35226
Phone: 205.979.9840
Fax: 205.979.5879
E-Mail: *alabama@hcrnetwork.com*

Arizona

Healthcare Recruiters of Phoenix
4545 East Shea Blvd.
Suite 209
Phoenix, AZ 85028
Phone: 602.494.9468
Fax: 602.494.0220
E-Mail: *phoenix@hcrnetwork.com*

Personnel Solutions
P.O. Box 32963
Phoenix, AZ 85064
Phone: 480.946.0999
Fax: 480.990.2045
E-Mail: *rick@personnelsols.com*
Internet: *http://www.personnelsols.com*

Work Wonders Staffing
4107 East Woodstock Rd.
Cave Creek, AZ 85331
Internet:
  http://www.workwondersstaffing.net

California

Agriesti & Associates
16291 Country Day Road
Poway, CA 92064
Phone: 858.451.7766
Fax: 858.451.7843
E-mail: *salesjob@san.rr.com*

Allen-Jeffers Associates
28512 Las Arubas
Laguna Niguel, CA 92677
Phone: 949.643.2146
Fax: 949.643.8476
E-mail: *contact@allen-jefferassociates.com*

Bayland Associates
4286 Redwood
Hwy 342
San Rafael, CA 94903
Phone: 415.499.8111
Fax: 415.499.8111
E-Mail: *baylandtjk@aol.com*

The Culver Group
6610 Flanders Dr.
San Diego, CA 92121
Internet: *http://www.culvercareers.com*
Multiple locations nationwide

Edwards Search Group Inc
1804 Soscol Avenue
Suite 201
Napa, CA 94559
Phone: 707.253.9200
Fax: 707.253.9222
E-Mail: *kenn@edwardssg.com*
Internet: *http://www.edwardssg.com*

**Fortune Personnel
Consultants — San Diego**
332 Encinitas Boulevard
Suite 200
Encinitas, CA 92024
Phone: 760.944.8980
Fax: 760.944.0075
E-Mail: *info@fpcsandiego.com*
Internet: *http://www.fpcsandiego.com*

Frank Parillo & Associates
1801 East Heim Avenue
Suite 200
Orange, CA 92865–3020
Phone: 714.921.8008
1.888.503.8249
Fax: 714.921.8568
E-Mail: *fparrillo@pacbell.net*
Internet: *http://www.frankparillo.qpg.com*

Healthcare Recruiters of the Bay Area
220 Montgomery Street
Suite 969
San Francisco, CA 94104
Phone: 415.773.0333
Fax: 415.773.0331
E-Mail: *bayarea@hcrnetwork.com*

Healthcare Recruiters of Los Angeles
15300 Ventura Boulevard
Suite 207
Sherman Oaks, CA 91403
Phone: 818.981.9510
Fax: 818.981.9523
E-Mail: *la@hcrnetwork.com*

Healthcare Recruiters of Orange County
26361 Crown Valley Parkway
Suite 150
Mission Viejo, CA 92691
Phone: 949.367.7888
Fax: 949.367.7881
E-Mail: *orangecounty@hcrnetwork.com*

Healthcare Recruiters of San Diego
701 Palomar Airport Road
Suite 300
Carlsbad, CA 92009
Phone: 760.931.4790
Fax: 760.931.9979
E-Mail: *sandiego@hcrnetwork.com*

Kuhn Med-Tech Inc.
27128-B Paseo Espada
Suite #623
San Juan Capistrano, CA 92675
Phone: 949.496.3500
Fax: 949.496.1716
E-Mail: *resume@kuhnmed-tech.com*
Internet: *http://www.kuhnmed-tech.com*

**Management Recruiters
International of Fresno**
5715 North West Avenue
Suite 101
Fresno, CA 93711-2366
Phone: 209.432.3700
1.800.881.4139
Fax: 209.432.9937
E-Mail: *ron@mri-fresno.com*
Internet: *http://www.mri-fresno.com*

**Management Recruiters International
of San Luis Obispo**
7360 El Camino Real
Suite A
Atascadero, CA 93422
Phone: 1.800.462.8044
Fax: 805.462.8047
E-Mail: *recruiter@healthcare-exec.com*
Internet: *http://www.healthcare-exec.com*

Med Exec International
100 North Brand Boulevard
Suite 306-308
Glendale, CA 91203
Phone: 818.552.2036
1.800.507.5277
Fax: 818.552.2475
E-Mail: *info@medexecintl.com*
Internet: *http://www.medexecintl.com*

MSI International
4275 Executive Square Drive
Suite 800
La Jolla, CA 92037
Phone: 1.800.859.5222
Fax: 619.546.2891
E-Mail: *mca@n2.net*
Internet: *http://www.msi-intl.com/mca*

National Career Choices
1300 B Santa Barbara Street
Santa Barbara, CA 93101
Phone: 1.800.622.0431
Fax: 805.966.9857
E-Mail: *ncc@nccx.com*

National Search Associates
2035 Corte del Nogal
Suite 100
Carlsbad, CA 92009
Phone: 760.431.1115
Fax: 760.431.0660
E-Mail: *bionsa@nsasearch.com*
Internet: *http://www.nsasearch.com*

Recruitment Resources Inc
2005 W. Culver Avenue
Suite 25
Orange, CA 92868
Phone: 714.978.7383
Fax: 714.978.7386
E-Mail: *pharmsearch@msn.com*

Sales Consultants of Chico
55 Independence Circle
Suite 108
Chico, CA 95973
Phone: 530.892.8880
Fax: 530.896.5480
E-Mail: *kl@medicaljobs.com*
Internet: *http://www.medicaljobs.com*

**Sanford Rose Associates —
Laguna Beach**
9 St. Francis Court
Suite D
Monarch Beach, CA 92629
Phone: 949.487.9055
Fax: 949.487.9214
E-Mail: *see web site*
Internet: *http://www.sralaguna.com*

TempTech
1223 Wilshire Blvd.
#841
Santa Monica, CA 90403
Phone: 310.395.4497
Fax: 310.362.8859
E-Mail: *Info@temptech.net*
Internet: *http://www.temptech.net*

Tumminelli and Associates
24988 Blue Ravine Road
Suite 108
Folsom, CA 95630
Phone: 916.353.1548
Fax: 916.353.2731
Email: *petet@medrecruitusa.com*
Internet: *http://www.medrecruitusa.com*

Canada

Brethet, Barnum & Associates Inc
703 Evans Ave
Suite 300
Toronto, ON M9C 5E9 Canada
Phone: 416.621.4900
Fax: 416.621.9818
E-Mail: *bshiley@wwonline.com*

Colorado

Fortune Personnel Consultants
Denver Office
7800 South Elati Street
Suite 319
Littleton, CO 80120
Phone: 303.795.9210
Fax: 303.795.9215
E-Mail: *mail@fpcdenver.com*
Internet: *http://www.fpcdenver.com*

Fortune Personnel Consultants — Golden
390 Union Blvd., Suite 250
Lakewood, CO 80228
Phone: 303.989.1544
Fax: 303.989.1506
E-Mail: *fpcgolden@uswest.net*
Internet:
  http://www.concentric.net/~fpcgolden

Healthcare Recruiters of the Rockies
6860 South Yosemite Court
Suite 2000
Englewood, CO 80112
Phone: 303.779.8570
Fax: 303.779.7974
E-Mail: *info@hcrrockies.com*
          rockies@hcrnetwork.com
Internet: *http://www.hcrrockies.com*

Connecticut

The Cambridge Group
1175 Post Road East
Westport, CT 06880
Phone: 1.800.525.3396
Fax: 203.226.3856
Internet: *http://www.cambridgegroup.com*

Florida

Absolute Recruiting Solutions, Inc (ARS)
Orlando, Florida
Phone: 407.880.2383
Fax: 407.880.8987
E-mail:
  info@absoluterecruitingsolutions.com
  resume@absoluterecruitingsolutions.com

Alexander Michaels Associates, Inc
107 Shadow Creek Way
Suite 105
Ormond Beach, FL 32174
Phone: 1.800.767.9988
Fax: 1.800.249.5683
Internet: *http://www.pharmsales.com*
E-mail: *larry@pharmsales.com*

American Recruiters Consolidated, Inc
6400 N. Andrews Avenue
Suite 120
Ft. Lauderdale, FL 33069
Phone: 954.492.4651
Fax: 954.492.4602
E-Mail: *glantz@arcimail.com*
Internet: *http://www.americanrecruiters.com*

The Bentley Group
2240 Woolbright Road
Suite 353
Boynton Beach, FL 33426
Phone: 561.734.3550
Fax: 561.734.3449
E-Mail: *info@bentleygrp.com*
Internet: *http://www.bentleygrp.com*

BioPharmMed
550 North Reo Street
Suite 300
Tampa, FL 33609
Phone: 813.261.5117
Fax: 813.805.0502
E-Mail: *bpm@ix.netcom.com*
Internet: *http://www.biopharmmed.com*

Career Search Group
1301 Seminole Boulevard
Suite 128
Largo, FL 33770
Phone: 727.586.2892
Fax: 727.584.6323
E-Mail: *careersearchgroup@hotmail.com*

Careerwise
8571 NW 11th Street
Coral Springs, FL 33071
Phone: 1.888.346.7560
Fax: 954.345.7701

Clinton, Charles, Wise & Company
931 State Road 434
Suite 1201–319
Altamonte Springs, FL 32714
Phone: 407.682.6790
Fax: 407.682.1697
E-Mail: *sales@recruitersofccwc.com*
Internet: *http://www.recruitersofccwc.com*

Healthcare Recruiters of Central Florida
215 Lincoln Avenue South
Clearwater, FL 33756
Phone: 727.467.9620
Fax: 727.467.9249
E-Mail: *tampa@hcrnetwork.com*

Hollters Group, International
2413 SW Parkside Drive
Palm City, FL 34990
Phone: 772.287.9689
Fax: 561.287.9603
E-Mail: *lois@hgint.com*
Internet: *http://www.hgint.com*

Karp & Associates
931 S R 434
Suite 1201
PMB 334
Altamonte Springs, FL 32714-7050
Phone: 407.292.4637
Fax: 407.294.1695
E-Mail: *lindakarp2@juno.com*

Mankuta, Gallagher & Associates, Inc.
8333 West McNabb Road
Suite 231
Ft. Lauderdale, FL 33321
Phone: 954.720.9645
Fax: 954.720.5813
E-Mail: *info@mankutagallagher.com*
        emankuta@mankutagallagher.com
Internet: *http://www.mankutagallagher.com*

Manny Barrientos
13400 Sutton Park Drive South
Suite 1601
Jacksonville, FL 32224
Phone: 904.398.9080 ext. 210
Fax: 904.398.8121
E-Mail: *manuelb1@aol.com*
Internet: *http://www.wolfganggroup.com*

Sales Consultants of St. Petersburg
275 104th Avenue
Unit A
Treasure Island, FL 33706
Phone: 727.367.8787
E-Mail: *scstpete1g@netscape.net*
Internet: *http://www.mrinet.com*

Georgia

Grobard & Associates Inc
230 Ridge Bluff Lane
Suwanee, GA 30024
Phone: 770.271.1828
Fax: 770.271.4026
E-Mail: *cygrob@charter.net*

Healthcare Recruiters of Atlanta
800 Old Roswell Lakes Parkway
Suite 160
Roswell, GA 30076
Phone: 770.640.8681
Fax: 770.640.9048
E-Mail: *atlanta@hcrnetwork.com*

**Management Recruiters
International of Atlanta Downtown, Inc**
230 Peachtree Street NW
Suite 1985
Atlanta, GA 30303
Phone: 404.221.1021
Fax: 404.221.0121
E-Mail: *jobs@mriatl.com*
Internet: *http://www.mriatl.com*

MSI International
2500 Marquis One Tower
245 Peachtree Center Avenue
Atlanta, GA 30303
Phone: 404.659.5050
Fax: 404.659.7139
E-Mail: *info@msi-intl.com*
Internet: *http://www.msi-intl.com*
(Many locations)

Salesforce
3294 Woodrow Way
Atlanta, GA 30319
Phone: 404.252.8566
Fax: 404.257.9312
E-Mail: *fred@shankweiler.com*
Internet: *http://www.shankweiler.com*

Illinois

A D Schiff & Associates, Ltd
869 Creek Bend Drive
Vernon Hills, IL 60061
Phone: 847.821.9220
Fax: 847.821.9298
E-Mail: *adschiff@theramp.net*

Executive Recruiting Associates
750 West Lake Cook Road
Suite 155
Buffalo Grove, IL 60089
Phone: 847.465.1020
Fax: 847.465.1546
E-Mail: *info@erecruitusa.com*
Internet: *http://www.erecruitusa.com*

Harbeck Associates
2003 Claremont Commons
Normal, IL 61761
Phone: 309.454.2456
Fax: 309.454.2774
Internet: *http://www.harbeckassociates.com*

HCI Corp.
29W585 Batavia Road
Warrenville, IL 60555
Phone: 630.393.6400
Fax: 630.393.6864
Internet: *http://www.healthcare-search.com*

Healthcare Recruiters of Chicago
850 North Milwaukee Avenue
Suite 204
Vernon Hills, IL 60061
Phone: 847.549.5885
Fax: 847.549.1570
E-Mail: *chicago@hcrnetwork.com*

Management Recruiters International of Lincolnshire-Buffalo Grove
1110 West Lake Cook Road
Suite 167
Buffalo Grove, IL 60089
Phone: 847.520.0107
E-Mail: *colnshire@earthlink.net*
Internet: *http://www.brilliantpeople.com*

Medical Sales Associates, Inc.
825 East Rand Road
Arlington Heights, IL

Medical Sales Associates
825 E Rand Road
Arlington Heights, IL 60004

Indiana

Healthcare Recruiters of Indiana
11550 North Meridian Street
Suite 210
Carmel, Indiana 46032
Phone: 317.843.5522
Fax: 317.843.5490
E-Mail: *jaclark@employusa.com*
         Indiana@hcrnetwork.com
Internet: *http://www.employusa.com*

Iowa

Sedona Staffing Services
3392 Hillcrest Road
Dubuque, IA 52002
Phone: 319.556.3040
Fax: 319.556.3041
E-Mail: *info@careerpros.com*
Internet: *http://www.careerpros.com*
(Several locations)

Kansas

The Chase Group
10955 Lowell Avenue
Suite 500
Overland Park, KS 66210
Phone: 913.663.3100
Fax: 913.663.3131
E-Mail: *chase@chasegroup.com*
Internet: *http://www.chasegroup.com*

Maine

The Auburn Group
One Wakefield Street
Suite 200
Lewiston, ME 04240
Phone: 207.753.6700
Fax: 207.753.0400
Internet: *http://www.theauburngroup.com*

The Haystack Group, Inc.
Submit Resume if you have prior Pharm.
  Sales Experience
15 High Street
P.O. Box 823
Vinalhave, Maine 04863–0823
Phone: 207.863.2793
Fax: 207.863.9916
E-Mail: *islandman@haystack-group.com*
Internet: *http://www.haystack-group.com*

Maryland

Craig Roe & Associates LLC
3711 Ashley Way
Suite A
Owings Mills, MD 21117
Phone: 410.654.6636
Fax: 410.654.6630
E-Mail: *sylvia@craigroeassocs.com*
Internet: *http://www.craigroeassocs.com*

Fortune Personnel Consultants — Baltimore
10 Crossroads Drive
Suite 201
Owings Mills, MD 21117
Phone: 410.581.0012
Fax: 410.581.2280
E-Mail: *execsearch@fpcbalt.com*
Internet: *http://www.fpcbalt.com*

Healthcare Recruiters of Mid Atlantic
4500 Black Rock Road
Suite 102
Hampstead, MD 21074
Phone: 410.239.6464
Fax: 410.374.5887
E-Mail: *midatlantic@hcrnetwork.com*

Mackenzie Search Group
939-I Beards Hill Road
Aberdeen, Maryland 21001
Phone: 410.942.0096
Fax: 410.942.0094
E-Mail: *info@msgsearch.com*
Internet: *http://www.MSGSearch.com*

Wasserman Associates
19 Raisin Tree Circle
Baltimore, MD 21208
Phone: 1.800.803.0011
Email: *careers@wassermanassociates.com*
Internet:
  http://www.wassermanassociates.com

Louisiana

Healthcare Recruiters of New Orleans
3500 North Causeway Boulevard
Suite 160
Metairie, LA 70002
Phone: 504.838.8875
Fax: 504.838.9962
E-Mail: *neworleans@hcrnetwork.com*

Innovative Medical Recruiting, LLC
221 Gum Bayou Lane
Slidell, LA 70461
Phone: 985.641.8817
Fax: 504.281.0118
E-Mail: *dale@innomedical.com*
Internet: *http://www.innomedical.com*

Massachusetts

BioWorks, Inc
7 Harris Avenue
Boston, MA 02130
Phone: 617.522.8618
Fax: 617.983.0624
www.jobscience.com

Fortune Personnel Consultants – Boston
100 Corporate Place
Suite 200
Peabody, MA 01960
Phone: 978.535.9920
Fax: 978.535.4482

Healthcare Recruiters of New England
1 Newbury Street
3rd Floor
Peabody, MA 01960
Phone: 978.535.3302
Fax: 978.535.3677
E-Mail: *newengland@hcrnetwork.com*

J. Robert Scott
260 Franklin St.
Suite 620
Boston, MA 02109
Phone: 617.563.2770
Fax: 617.723.1282
E-Mail: *resumes@j-robert-scott.com*
Internet: *http://www.j-robert-scott.com*

Positions Incorporated
South One Faneuil Marketplace
5th Floor
Boston, MA 21090
Phone: 617.367.9200
Fax: 617.367.4906
E-Mail: *positionsinc@worldnet.att.net*
Internet: *http://www.positionsinc.com*

Resource Inc
P.O. Box 420
Marshfield Hills, MA 02051
Phone: 781.837.8113
Fax: 781.837.8063
E-Mail: *resume@tchresource.com*
Internet: *http://www.tchresource.com*

Treeline Inc.
591 North Avenue
Suite #2
Wakefield, MA 01880
Phone: 781.224.9696
Fax: 781.224.9797
Email: *Sales@treeline-inc.com*
Internet: *http://www.treeline-inc.com*

Michigan

Healthcare Recruiters of Michigan
10327 East Grand
Suite 409
Brighton, MI 48116
Phone: 810.227.7055
Fax: 810.227.7307
E-Mail: *michigan@hcrnetwork.com*

Minnesota

Healthcare Recruiters of Minnesota
18315 Cascade Drive
Suite 190
Eden Prairie, MN 55347
Phone: 952.975.4981
Fax: 509.691.8232
E-Mail: *minnesota@hcrnetwork.com*

Missouri

Healthcare Recruiters of Mid America
10920 Ambassador Drive
Suite 320
Kansas City, MO 64153
Phone: 816.891.7778
Fax: 816.891.7377
E-Mail: *midamerica@hcrnetwork.com*

Healthcare Recruiters of St. Louis
15400 South Outer Forty
Suite 100
Chesterfield, MO 63017
Phone: 636.530.1030
Fax: 636.530.1039
E-Mail: *stlouis@hcrnetwork.com*

Jim Crumpley & Associates
1200 East Woodhurst Drive
Bldg. B, Suite 400
Springfield, MO 65804
Phone: 417.882.7555
Fax: 417.882.8555
E-Mail: *recruiter@crumpleyjobs.com*
Internet: *http://www.crumpleyjobs.com*

Med-Search Recruiting Network, Inc.
15933 Clayton Rd.
St. Louis, MO 63011
Phone: 636.230.0717
Fax: 636.230.9483
Internet: *http://www.medrecruiters.com*

Select Medical Solutions
16303 Autumn View Terrace
St. Louis, MO 63011
Phone: 636.405.0333
Fax: 636.458.4657
E-Mail: *steve@selectmedicalsolutions.com*

Montana

Fortune Personnel Consultants — Bozeman
104 E. Main Street
Suite 302
Bozeman, MT 59715
Phone: 406.585.1332
Fax: 406.585.2255
E-Mail: *fpcbozeman@mcn.net*
Internet: *http://www.fpcweb.com*

Harbrowe Inc
P.O. Box 1240
Marion, MT 59925
Phone: 1.877.964.7301
Fax: 406.854.2320
E-Mail: *j@harbrowe.com*
Internet: *http://www.harbrowe.com*
www.greatsalesjobs.com

New Jersey

Besen Associates
PO Box 57
Lake Hiawatha, NJ 07034
Phone: 973.334.5533
Fax: 973.334.4810
E-Mail: *besenassoc@aol.com*
Internet: *http://www.besen.com*

The Cassie Group
26 Main Street
Toms River, NJ 08753
Phone: 732.473.1779
E-Mail: *cassiegroup@cassie.com*
Internet: *http://www.cassie.com*

Headhunters Executive Search Inc
96 Princeton Street
Nutley, NJ 07110
Phone: 973.667.2799
E-Mail: *medsalesplus@aol.com*

Healthcare Recruiters of New York, New Jersey
55 Harristown Road
Glen Rock, NJ 07452
Phone: 201.670.9800
Fax: 201.670.1908
E-Mail: *nynj@hcrnetwork.com*

Healthcare Recruiters of Philadelphia
3 Eves Drive
Suite 303
Marlton, NJ 08053
Phone: 856.596.7179
Fax: 856.596.6895
E-Mail: *philadelphia@hcrnetwork.com*

Ken Clark Int'l
2000 Lenox Drive
Suite 200
Lawrenceville, NJ 08648
Phone: 609.308.5200
Fax: 609.308.5250
E-Mail: *info@kenclark.com*
Internet: *http://www.kenclark.com*
(Multiple locations)

Kingsley Quinn/USA
PO Box 5155
Basking Ridge, NJ 07920
Phone: 908.580.1688
Fax: 908.580.0163
E-Mail: *kqusa@kingsleyquinn.com*

The Normyle/Erstling Health Search Group
350 West Passaic Street
Rochelle Park, NJ 07662
Fax: 201.843.2060
E-Mail: *jobs@medpharmsales.com*
Internet: *http://www.medpharmsales.com*

Ogilvie-Smartt Associates, LLC
23 Davenport Way
Hillsborough, NJ 08844
Phone: 908.359.8319
Fax: 610.469.0413
E-Mail: *rudy.smartt@osasearch.com*
Internet: *http://www.osasearch.com*

Pharmaceutical Clinical Associates, LLC
P.O. Box 2586
Trenton, NJ 08690
Phone: 609.586.4141
Fax: 609.586.1987
E-Mail: *pharmca@aol.com*
Internet: *http://www.pharmca.com*

Ruderfer & Company, Inc
908 Pompton Avenue
Suite A-2
Cedar Grove, NJ 07009
Phone: 973.857.2400
Fax: 973.857.4343
E-Mail: *search@ruderfer.com*

Sales Consultants of Cherry Hill
800 North Kings Highway
Suite 402
Cherry Hill, NJ 08034-1511
Phone: 856.779.9100
Fax: 856.779.9193
E-Mail: *sccherryhill@aol.com*
Internet: *http://www.mriphiladelphia.com*

SMR Group Limited
200 Sheffield Street
Suite 308
Mountainside, NJ 07092
Phone: 1.800.767.3340
Fax: 908.789.2080
E-Mail: *see web site*
Internet: *http://www.smrgroupltd.com*

New Hampshire

Barrett & Company Inc
59 Stiles Road
Suite 105
Salem, NH 03079
Phone: 603.890.1111
Fax: 603.890.1118
E-Mail:
 barrettcompany@barrettcompany.com
Internet: *http://www.barrettcompany.com*

Fortune Personnel
 ### Consultants — Nashua
505 West Hollis,
Suite 208
Nashua, NH 03062
Phone: 603.880.8880
Fax: 603.880.8861
E-Mail: *mail@fpcnashua.com*
Internet: *http://www.fpcnashua.com*

New York

Bornholdt Shivas & Friends
400 East 87th Street
New York, NY 10128-6533
Phone: 212.557.5252
Fax: 212.557.5704
E-Mail: *bsandf@aol.com*
Internet: *http://members.aol.com/bsandf*

Caplan Associates Inc
P.O. Box 4227
77 Bull Path
East Hampton, NY 11937
Phone: 631.907.9700
Fax: 631.907.0444
E-Mail: *info@caplanassoc.com*
Internet: *http://www.caplanassoc.com*
 http://www.caplanassoc.com

Career & Business Services
142 Route 306
Monsey, NY 10952
Phone: 845.371.5207
Fax: 845.425.8053

The Dartmouth Group
2500 Johnson Avenue
Suite 16N
Riverdale, NY 10463
Phone: 718.884.2411
Fax: 718.884.3025
E-Mail: *sales@dartmouthgroup.com*

The Hampton Group
33 Flying Point Road
Southampton, NY 11968
Phone: 631.287.3330
Fax: 631.287.5610
www.hamptongrp.com

Healthcare Recruiters of New York
455 Electronics Parkway
Building 2, Suite 208
Liverpool, NY 13088
Phone: 315.453.4080
Fax: 315.453.9525
E-Mail: *newyork@hcrnetwork.com*

Pharmaceutical Careers Inc
P.O. Box 124
Pleasantville, NY 10570
Phone: 914.769.1400
Fax: 914.769.1496
E-Mail: *mail@pharmaceuticalcareers.com*
Internet:
 http://www.pharmaceuticalcareers.com

Sales Source
331 Ushers Road
Ballston Lake, NY 12019
Phone: 518.877.6706
1.800.229.3093
Fax: 518.877.8161
E-Mail: *home@salessource.net*
Internet: *http://www.salessource.net*

North Carolina

The Everhart Group
2121 Eastchester Drive
Suite 101
High Point, NC 27265
Phone: 336.841.0123
Fax: 336.841.0047
Internet: *http://www.mreverhart.com*

Fortune Personnel
Consultants — Raleigh
7521 Mourning Dove Road
Suite 101
Raleigh, NC 27615
Phone: 919.848.9929
Fax: 919.848.1062
E-Mail: *info@fpcraleigh.com*
Internet: *http://www.fpcraleigh.com*

Healthcare Recruiters of the Carolinas
535 Keisler Drive
Suite 202
Cary, NC 27511
Phone: 919.858.7017
Fax: 919.858.7018
E-Mail: *carolinas@hcrnetwork.com*

Pat Licata & Associates
103 Quarterpath Drive
Cary, NC 27511
Phone: 919.859.3203
Fax: 919.653.1199
E-Mail: *see web site*
Internet: *http://www.patlicata.com*

Phil Ellis Associates Inc
PO Box 900
Wrightsville Beach, NC 28480
Phone: 910.256.9810
Fax: 910.256.9887
E-Mail: *philellis@pellis.com*
Internet: *http://www.pellis.com*

Ohio

Baldwin & Associates
3975 Erie Avenue
Cincinnati, OH 45208–1908
Phone: 513.272.2400
Fax: 513.527.5929
E-Mail: *office@baldwin-assoc.com*
Internet: *http://www.baldwin-assoc.com*

Healthcare Recruiters of Cincinnati
10 North Locust Street
Suite C-1
Oxford, OH 45056
Phone: 513.523.8004
Fax: 513.523.9004
E-Mail: *ohio@hcrnetwork.com*

The Hogan Group Inc
12434 Cedar Rd.
Cleveland Heights, OH 44106
Phone: 216.421.9507
E-Mail: *thehogangp@aol.com*
Internet: *http://www.thehogangroup.net*

Mars Employment Inc.
5813 Mayfield Road
205
Mayfield Heights, Ohio 44124
Phone: 1.800.253.8456

Richard Kader & Associates
6777 Engle Road
Suite A
Cleveland, OH 44130
Phone: 440.891.1700
Fax: 440.891.1443
Internet: *http://www.kaderonline.com*

Sanford Rose Associates
3737 Embassy Parkway
Akron, OH 44333-8369
Phone: 1.800.731.7724
Fax: 330.670.9798
E-Mail: *resumes@sanfordrose.com*
Internet: *http://www.sanfordrose.com*
(Multiple locations)

Oklahoma

Sales Recruiters of Oklahoma City
6803 South Western Avenue
Suite 305
Oklahoma City, OK 73139
Phone: 405.848.1536
E-Mail: *jr@salesrec.com*
Internet: *http://www.salesrec.com*

Pennsylvania

Century Associates Inc
1420 Walnut Street
Suite 1402
Philadelphia, PA 19102
Phone: 215.732.4311
Fax: 215.735.1804
E-Mail: *bcohen@centuryassociates.com*
Internet: *http://www.centuryassociates.com*

DiCenzo Personnel Specialists
428 Forbes Avenue
Suite 110
Pittsburgh, PA 15219
Phone: 412.281.6207
Fax: 412.281.9326
E-Mail: *dicenzo@usa.net*
Internet: *http://www.dicenzo.com*

**Fortune Personnel
Consultants — Abington**
1410 West Street Road
Warminster, PA 18974
Phone: 215.675.3100
Fax: 215.675.3080
E-Mail: *fpcabi@navpoint.com*

Healthcare Recruiters of Pittsburgh
600 Lawyers Building
428 Forbes Avenue
Pittsburgh, PA 15219
Phone: 412.261.2244
Fax: 412.261.3577
E-Mail: *pittsburgh@hcrnetwork.com*

Interactive Search Associates
2949 West Germantown Pike
Norristown, PA 19403
Phone: 610.630.3670
Fax: 610.630.3678
Internet: *http://www.zerkle.com*

International Pro Sourcing
407 Executive Drive
Langhorne, PA 19047
Phone: 215.968.7667
Fax: 215.968.7667
E-Mail: *admin@prosourcing.com*
Internet: *http://www.prosourcing.com*

Patriot Associates
125 Strafford Avenue
Suite 300
Wayne, PA 19087-3318
Phone: 610.687.7770
Fax: 610.975.4512
E-Mail: *tompatriot@aol.com*

Pharmaceutical Search Professionals Inc
311 N. Sumneytown Pike
Suite 1A
North Wales, PA 19454
Phone: 215.699.1900
Fax: 215.699.9189
E-Mail: *pspi@pspisearch.com*
Internet:
  http://www.pharmaceutical-search.com

**Sales Consultants of
Chester County, PA**
5 Frame Avenue
Suite 101
Frame Avenue Business Complex
Malvern, PA 19355
Phone: 610.695.8420
Fax: 610.695.8442
E-Mail: *springco@erols.com*

South Carolina

**Fortune Personnel
Consultants — Anderson**
100 Miracle Mile Drive
Suite F
Anderson, SC 29621
Phone: 864.226.5322
Fax: 864.225.6767
E-Mail: *fpcabi@navpoint.com*
Internet: *http://www.fpcsearch.com*

**Fortune Personnel
Consultants — Charleston**
890 Johnnie Dodds Boulevard
Suite 202 , Building 3
P.O. Box 2544
Mount Pleasant, SC 29465-2544
Phone: 843.884.0505
Fax: 843.849.9522
E-Mail:
  recruiting.partners@fpccharleston.com
Internet: *http://www.fpccharleston.com*

**Fortune Personnel
Consultants — Hilton Head**
52 New Orleans Road
Suite 201–Jade Building
Hilton Head Island, SC 29928
Phone: 843.842.7221
Fax: 843.842.7205
E-Mail: *recruit@fpchh.com*
Internet: *http://www.fpchh.com*

Tennessee

Healthcare Recruiters of the Mid South
356 New Byhalia Road
Suite 1
Collierville, TN 38017
Phone: 901.853.0900
Fax: 901.853.6500
E-Mail: *midsouth@hcrnetwork.com*

Management Recruiters Chattanooga-Brainerd, Inc.
Sales Consultants
6005 Century Oaks Drive
Suite 400
Chattanooga, TN 37416
423-894-5500
423-894-1177 FAX
E-Mail: *resume@mrichattanooga.com*
Internet: *http://www.mrichattanooga.com*

Sales Consultants of Chattanooga-Brainerd
7010 Lee Highway
Suite 216
Chattanooga, TN 37421
Phone: 423.894.5500
Fax: 423.894.1177
E-Mail: *mrichatt@cdc.net*
Internet: *http://www.mrichattanooga.com*

SalesHunter, Inc
P.O. Box 38328
Memphis, TN 38183-0328
Phone: 901.751.1995
E-Mail: *info@saleshunter.com*
Internet: *http://www.saleshunter.com*

Texas

Fortune Personnel Consultants — North Dallas
1545 W. Mockingbird Lane
Suite 1020
Dallas, TX 75232
Phone: 214.634.3929
Fax: 214.634.7741
E-Mail: *info@fpcndallas.com*
Internet: *http://www.fpcndallas.com*

Fortune Personnel Consultants — San Antonio
10924 Vance Jackson
Suite 303
San Antonio, TX 78230
Phone: 210.696.9797
Fax: 210.696.6909
E-Mail: *fpcsat@fpcsat.com*
Internet: *http://www.fpcsat.com*

Healthcare Recruiters International
Corporate Office
5220 Spring Valley Road
Suite 40
Dallas, TX 75240
Phone: 972.702.0444
Fax: 972.702.0432
E-Mail: *corp@hcrnetwork.com*
Internet: http://www.hcrintl.com

Healthcare Recruiters of Dallas
4100 Spring Valley Road
Suite 800
Dallas, TX 75244
Phone: 214.420.9370
Fax: 214.420.9334
E-Mail: *dallas@hcrnetwork.com*

Kaye/Bassman International
18333 Preston Road
Suite 500
Dallas, TX 75252
Phone: 972.931.5242
Fax: 972.931.9683
E-Mail: *kbic@kbic.com*
Internet: *http://www.kbic.com*

Lord & Albus
10314 Sweet Wood Drive
Houston, TX 77070
Phone: 281.955.5673
Fax: 281.955.7096

MedSource
1225 Precinct Line Road
Suite R
Hurst, TX 76053
Phone: 817.284.8886
Fax: 817.284.3465

Virginia

Management Recruiters International of Piedmont
Route 7 Box 7327
Palmyra, VA 22963
Phone: 434.591.1028
1.800.976.1972
Fax: 434.591.1139
E-Mail: *rxsales@cstone.net*
Internet: *http://www.pharmarecruiting.com*

Washington

BPM Recruiters
P.O. Box 3738
Silverdale, WA 98383
Phone: 360.308.0038
Fax: 360.598.2979
bpmrecruiters@aol.com

Fortune Personnel Consultants
East Seattle Office
11661 SE 1st Street
Suite 202
Bellevue, WA 98005
Phone: 425.450.9665
Fax: 425.450.0357
E-Mail: *info@fpc-eastseattle.com*
Internet: *http://www.fpc-eastseattle.com*

Healthcare Recruiters of the Northwest
321 Park Place
Suite G-116
Kirkland, WA 98033
Phone: 425.576.5115
Fax: 425.576.5225
E-Mail: *northwest@hcrnetwork.com*

Management Recruiters International of Vancouver
703 Broadway Street
Suite 695
Vancouver, WA 98660
Phone: 360.695.4688
Fax: 360.695.4384
E-Mail: *jpoloni@mrvancouver.com*
Internet: *http://www.mrvancouver.com*

Sales Talent, Inc
270 3rd Avenue
Suite 200
Kirkland, WA 98033
Phone: 425.739.9979
Fax: 425.828.3861
E-Mail: *yaffa@salestalentinc.com*
Internet: *http://www.salestalentinc.com*

Washington DC

Positions Incorporated
919 Eighteenth Street
Suite 230
Washington DC 20006
Phone: 202.657.9270
Fax: 202.657.9245
Internet: *http://www.positionsinc.com*

Wisconsin

Healthcare Recruiters of Wisconsin
405 Forest Street
Oconomowoc, WI 53066
Phone: 414.569.6747
Fax: 414.569.6749
E-Mail: *wisconsin@hcrnetwork.com*

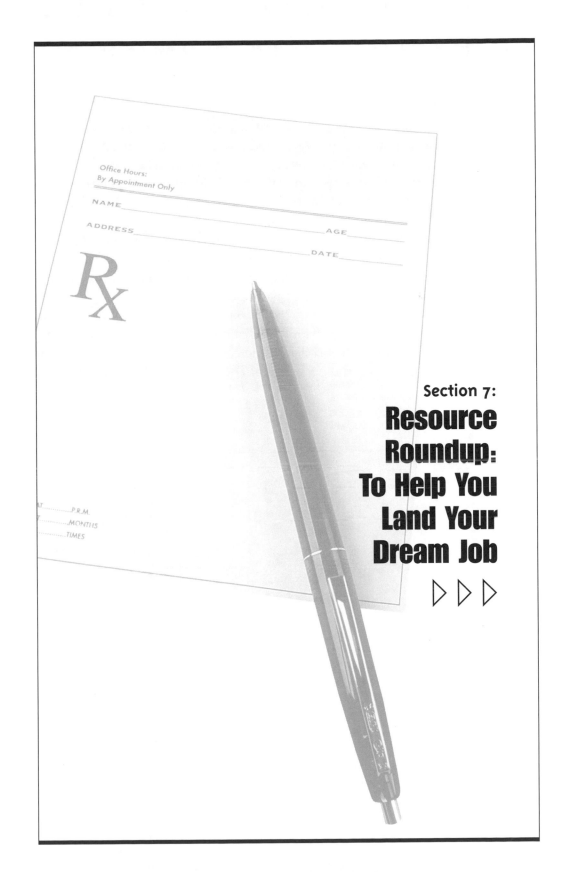

Office Hours:
By Appointment Only

NAME

ADDRESS   AGE

                                           DATE

℞

...P.R.M.

...MONTHS

...TIMES

Section 7:
Resource Roundup: To Help You Land Your Dream Job

▷ ▷ ▷

RESOURCE ROUNDUP: TO HELP YOU LAND YOUR DREAM JOB

Pharmaceutical Company Contact List:

The following is a list of some of the key pharmaceutical companies in North America. It is not a comprehensive list. Keep in mind that due to mergers and acquisitions, companies are changing all the time. The contact names and numbers may have changed since this publishing. Also, remember that most of these companies are very large and have locations worldwide.

If you plan to apply to any of these companies, you will be most successful by posting your résumé directly on their website. Doing this usually helps your résumé get floated to several of their divisions for consideration. If you were to mail a résumé, it may not get as much exposure.

Note: Some of the Canadian divisions of US companies are listed individually. If you don't see the division listed, the contact information for careers can most often be found on the US website. The same goes for other international locations.

3m United States
3m H/S
575 West Murray Blvd.
Murray, UT 84123
Phone: 1 (888) 364-3577

Abbott Laboratories
100 Abbott Park Rd.
Abbott Park, IL 60064-3500
Phone: (847) 937-6100
http://www.abbott.com

Alcon Laboratories
6201 S Freeway
Fort Worth, TX 76134
Phone: (817) 293-0450
http://www.alconlabs.com

Allergan
255 DuPont Drive
Irvine, CA 92612
Phone: (714) 246-4500
http://www.allergan.com

Altana Pharmaceuticals Inc., Canada
7435 N Service Road West, 1st floor
Oakville, ON 48X CA
Phone: (905) 469-9333
email: *careers@altanapharma.ca*
http://www.altanapharma.ca

Amgen Inc.
One Amgen Center Drive
Thousand Oaks, CA 91320
Phone: (805) 447-1000

Ascent Pediatrics
187 Ballardvale Street
Wilmington, MA 01887
Phone: (978) 658-2500
http://www.ascentpediatrics.com

AstraZeneca
1800 Concord Pike
Wilmington, DE 19850-F315
Phone: (800) 456-3669
http://www.astrazeneca-us.com

Aventis Pharmaceuticals
300 Somerset Corporate Boulevard
Bridgewater, NJ 08807-2854
Phone: (800) 981-2491
http://www.aventis.com

Axcan Pharma Inc. (Canada)
597 Laurier Blvd
Mont Saint Hilaire, QC J3H 6C4 CA
Phone: (450) 467-5138
http://www.axcan.com

Axcan Pharma Inc. (US)
Sandi Howard
Employment Manager
Axcan Scandipharm Inc.
Fax: (205) 991-0639

Berlex Labs
340 Changebridge Rd.
Box 1000
Montville, NJ 07045
Phone: (973) 487-2000
http://www.berlex.com

Bertek Pharmaceuticals Inc.
781 Chestnut Ridge Rd.
Morgantown, NV 26505
Phone: (888) 823-7835
http://www.bertek.com

Bradley Pharmaceuticals, Inc.
383 Rt. 46 West
Fairfield, NJ 07004
E-Mail: *personnel@bradpharm.com*
http://www.bradpharm.com

Biovail Pharmaceuticals Inc.
7150 Mississauga Road
Mississauga, Ontario
Canada L5N 8M5
Phone: (905) 286-3000
http://www.biovailpharm.com

Boehringer Ingelheim Canada
5180 South Service Road
Burlington, ON L7L 5H4 CA
Phone: (905) 639-0333
http://www.boehringer-ingelheim.ca

Boehringer Ingelheim Corp.
900 Ridgebury Rd.
Ridgefield, CT 06877
Phone: (800) 542-6257
http://www.boehringer-ingelheim.com

Braintree Laboratories
60 Columbian Street West
PO Box 850929
Braintree, MA 02185-0929
Phone: (800) 874-6756
http://www.braintreelabs.com

Bristol-Meyers Squibb Company
PO Box 5335
Princeton, NJ 08543
http://www.bms.com

Celltech Pharmaceuticals, Inc.
PO Box 31710
Rochester, NY 14603
Phone: (716) 475-9000
http://www.orgs.com

Chiron Corporation
4560 Horton Street
Emeryville, CA 94608
Phone: (510) 655-8730
http://www.chiron.com

Connetics Corporation
3290 West Bayshore Rd
Palo Alto, CA 94303-4013
Phone: (650) 843-2800
http://www.connetics.com

Daiichi Pharmaceutical Corporation
11 Phillips Parkway
Montvale, NJ 07645
Phone: (877) 324-4244
http://www.daiichius.com

Dermik Labs (division of Sanofi-Aventis)
500 Arcola Ln.
Collegeville, PA 19426-0107
Phone: (610) 454-8000
http://www.dermik.com

Dey Laboratories
2751 Napa Valley Corporate Dr.
Napa, CA 94558
Phone: (800) 869-9005
http://www.deyinc.com

Dupont Pharmaceuticals Company
Chestnut Run Place
Wilmington, DE 19805
Phone: (302) 992-5000
http://www.dupont.com

Eisai Inc.
500 Frank W. Burr Blvd.
Teaneck, NJ 07666-6741
Phone: (888) 274-2378
http://wwww.eisai.com

Elan Pharmaceuticals
800 Gateway Blvd.
South San Francisco, CA 94080
Phone: (650) 877-0900
http://www.elan.com

Eli Lilly and Company
Lilly Corporate Center
Indianapolis, IN 46285
Phone: (317) 276-2000
http://www.lilly.com

Endo Pharmaceuticals
Human Resources
100 Painters Drive
Chadds Ford, PA 19317
Phone: (610) 558-9800
http://www.endo.com

Ferndale Labratories Inc.
780 W Eight Mile Road
Ferndale, MI 48220
Phone: (248) 548-0900
http://www.ferndalelabs.com

Ferring Pharmaceuticals, Inc.
400 Rella Boulevard
Suite 300
Suffern, NY 10901
Phone: (845) 770-2600
http://www.ferringusa.com

First Horizon Pharmaceuticals Corp.
HR Dept.
6195 Shiloh Road
Alpharetta, GA 30005
http://www.horizonpharm.com

Forest Pharmaceuticals Inc.
909 Third Ave.
New York, NY 10022
Phone: (800) 947-5227
http://www.forestlabs.com

Fujisawa USA Inc
Attn. Human Resources
Three Parkway North
Deerfield, IL 60015
Phone: (847) 317-8800
http://www.fujisawa.com

Gate Pharmaceuticals (division of Tera Pharmaceuticals USA)
PO Box 1090
North Wales, PA 19454
Phone: (800) 292-4293
http://www.gatepharma.com

GlaxoSmithKline
Five Moore Dr.
Research Triangle Park, NC 27709
Phone: (888) 825-5249
http://www.gsk.com

Healthpoint Phamaceuticals
3909 Hullen Street
Fort Worth, TX 76107
Phone: (800) 441-8227
http://www.healthpoint.com

Hoechst Marion Roussel Canada Inc.
2150 Boul St. Elzear Boulevard
West Laval, Quebec H7L4A8 Canada
Phone: 0004180

Hoffman-la Roche Ltd. Canada
2455 Meadowpine Boulevard
Mississauga ON L5N6L7 Canada
http://www.roche.com

Hoffman-la Roche US
340 Kingsland Street
Nutley, NJ 07110
Phone: (973) 235-5000
http://www.rocheusa.com

Innovex
Waterview Corporate Centre
Parsippany, NJ 07054
Phone: (973) 257-4500
http://www.innovexglobal.com

Integrity Pharmaceutical Corporation
9084 Technology Drive
Fishers, IN 46038
Phone: (800) 823-6878
http://www.integritypharma.com

Ivax Corporation
4400 Biscayne Blvd
Miami, FL 33137
Phone: (800) 980-4829
http://www.ivax.com

Janssen Pharmaceutica (Division of Johnson and Johnson)
1125 Trenton-Harbourton Rd.
Titusville, NJ 08560-0200
Phone: (609) 730-2080
http://www.us.janssen.com

Johnson &Johnson
501 George St.
New Brunswick, NJ 08901
http://www.jnj.com/careers

Key Pharmaceuticals Inc. (Division of Schering-Plough, Inc.)
Galloping Hill Rd.
Kenilworth, NJ 07033
Phone: (908) 298-4000

King Pharmaceuticals, Inc.
501 5th Street
Bristol, TN 37620
http://www.kingpharm.com

Knoll Pharmaceutical Co.
3000 Continental Drive North
Mount Olive, NJ 07828-1234
Phone: (973) 428-4000

Leo Pharma
123 Commerce Valley Drive East,
  Suite 400
Thornhill, ON L3T 7W8 CA
Phone: (905) 886-9822
http://www.leo-pharma.com

Mead Johnson Nutritionals Canada
1 (800) 263-7464
http://www.meadjohnson.ca
email: *mjnjobs@bms.com*

McKesson
One Post Street
San Francisco, CA 94104-5296
Phone: (415) 983-8300
http://www.mckesson.com

McNeil Consumer Healthcare
7050 Camp Hill Road
Fort Washington, PA 19034
Phone: (215) 273-7000
http://www.mcneilcampusrecruiting.com

MedPointe Pharmaceuticals
265 Davidson Ave., Suite 300
Somerset, NJ 08873
Phone: (732) 564-2200
http://www.medpointepharma.com

Merck & Co., Inc.
1 Merck Drive
PO Box 100
Whitehouse Station, NJ 08889
Phone: (908) 423-1000
http://www.merck.com

MGI Pharma, Inc.
5775 West Old Shakopee Road
Suite 100
Bloomington, MN 55437
Phone: (612) 346-4700
http://www.mgipharma.com

Muro Pharmaceuticals Inc.
890 East St.
Tewksbury, MA 01876-1496
Phone: (800) 225-0974

Novartis Pharmaceuticals Corp.
59 Route 10
East Hanover, NJ 07936-1080
Phone: (888) 669-6682
http://www.novartis.com
hrjobs@novartis.com

Noven Pharmaceuticals
11960 SW 144th Street
Miami, FL 33186
Phone: (305) 253-5099
http://www.noven.com

Novo Nordisk Pharmaceuticals Inc.
100 College Road West
Princeton, NJ 08540
Phone: (609) 987-5800
http://www.novonordisk.com

Organon, Inc.
375 Mt. Pleasant Ave
West Orange, NJ 07052
Phone: (800) 241-8812
http://www.organon.com

Ortho Biotech Inc.
430 Route 22 East
Box 6914
Bridgewater, NJ 08807
Phone: (908) 541-4000
http://www.orthobiotech.com

Ortho McNeil Pharmaceutical
1000 Route 202 South
Raritan, NJ 08869-0602
Phone: (800) 682-6532
http://www.ortho-mcneil.com

Otsuka America Pharmaceutical Inc.
2440 Research Blvd.
Rockville, MD 20850
Phone: (301) 990-0030
http://www.otsuka.com

PediaMed Pharmaceuticals
7310 Turfway Road
Suite 490
Florence, KY 41042
Phone: (866) 543-6337
http://www.pediamedpharma.com

Pfizer Inc.
235 East 42nd St.
New York, NY 10017
Phone: (212) 733-2323
http://www.pfizer.com

Procter & Gamble Pharmaceuticals
One Proctor & Gamble Plaza
Cincinnati, OH 45202
Phone: (800) 448-4878
http://www.pg.com

Professional Detailing Inc.
Saddle River Executive Center
1 Route 17 South
Saddle River, NJ 07458
Phone: (201) 818-8450
http://www.pdi-inc.om

Purdue Pharma
One Stamford Forum
Stamford, CT 06901-3431
Phone: (203) 588-8000
http://www.purduepharma.com

Purdue Pharma Canada
Human Resources
575 Granite Court
Pickering Ontario L1w3w8 Canada
http://www.purdue.ca
email: *info@pfcan.com*

Ranbaxy Pharmaceuticals, Ltd.
600 College Road East
Suite 2100
Princeton, NJ 08540
Phone: (609) 720-9200
http://www.ranbaxyusa.com

Reliant Pharmaceuticals
110 Allen Road
Liberty Corner, NJ 07938
Phone: (908) 580-1200
http://www.reliantrx.com

Ross Products Division
625 Cleveland Ave
Columbus, OH 43215-1724
Phone: (800) 986-8510
http://www.ross.com

Salix Pharmaceuticals Ltd.
8540 Colonnade Center Drive
Raleigh, NC 27615
Phone: (919) 862-1000
http://www.salixltd.com

Sankyo Pharma
Two Hilton Court
Parsippany, NJ 07054
Phone: (973) 359-2600
http://www.sankyopharma.com

Sanofi-Aventis
90 Park Ave
New York, NY 10016
Phone: (212) 551-4000
http://www.sanofi-synthelabo.com

Santen, Inc.
555 Gateway Drive
Napa, CA 94558
Phone: (707) 254-1750
http://www.santen.com

Savage Laboratories
60 Baylis Rd.
Melville, NY 11747
Phone: (800) 231-0206
http://www.savagelabs.com

Schering-Plough Corp.
2000 Galloping Hill Road
Kenilworth, NJ 07033
Phone: (973) 298-4000
http://www.schering-plough.com

Schwarz Pharma Inc.
PO Box 2038
Milwaukee, WI 53201
Phone: (800) 558-5114
http://www.schwarzusa.com

Sepracor Inc.
84 Waterford Drive
Marlborough, MA 01752
Phone: (508) 481-6700
http://www.sepracor.com

Serono Inc.
One Technology Place
Rockland, MA 02370
Phone: (800) 283-8088
http://www.seronousa.com

Servier Canada, Inc.
235 Blvd Armand-Frappier
Laval, QC H7V4A7 CA
Phone: (450) 978-9700
http://www.servier.com

Shire Richwood Pharmaceuticals
7900 Tanners Gate Dr
Florence, KY 41042
Phone: (859) 282-2100
http://www.shiregroup.com

Sigma Tau Pharmaceuticals
800 South Frederick Av.
Gaithersburg, MD 20877
Phone: (301) 948-1041
http://www.sigmatau.com

Solvay Pharmaceuticals Inc.
901 Sawyer Rd.
Marietta, GA 30062
Phone: (770) 578-9000
http://www.solvaypharmaceuticals-us.com

Stiefel Laboratories Inc
255 Alhambra Circle
Coral Gables, FL 33134
Phone: (888) 784-3335
http://www.stiefel.com

Stiefel Canada
6635 Henri-Bourassa Boulevard West
Montreal H4R1E1 Quebec Canada
Phone: 1(800) 363-2862
http://www.stiefel.ca

Takeda Pharmaceuticals America Inc
475 Half Day Road
Lincolnshire, IL 60069
Phone: (847) 383-3000
http://www.takedapharm.com

TAP Pharmaceutical Products Inc
675 North Field Drive
Lake Forest, IL 60045
Phone: (800) 621-1020
http://www.tap.com

Teva USA
1090 Horsham Road
PO Box 1090
North Wales, PA 19454
Phone: (215) 591-3000
http://tevapharmusa.com

UCB Pharma Inc.
1950 Lake Park Dr.
Smyrna, GA 30080
Phone: (800) 477-7877
http://www.ucbpharma.com

Upsher-Smith Laboratories, Inc.
6701 Evanstad Dr.
Maple Grove, MN 55369
Phone: (800) 654-2299
http://www.upsher-smith.com

Valeant Pharmaceuticals International
3300 Hyland Ave.
Costa Mesa, CA 97626
Phone: 1 (800) 548-5100
http://www.valeant.com

Warner Chilcott
Rockaway 80 Corporate Center
Rockaway, NJ 07886
Phone: (973) 442-3200
http://www.wclabs.com

Watson Pharmaceuticals
311 Bonnie Circle
Corona, CA 92880
Phone: (800) 272-5525
http://www.watsonpharm.com

Womens First Healthcare
12220 El Camino Real, Suite 400
San Diego, CA 92130
Phone: (858) 509-1171
http://www.womensfirst.com

Wyeth Laboratories
5 Giralda Farms
Madison, NJ 07940
Phone: (610) 902-1200
http://www.wyeth.com

CONTRACT PHARMACEUTICAL COMPANIES

Contract staffing companies provide sales forces and managers for some of the top pharmaceutical companies. Pharmaceutical companies in need of a "temporary" increase in sales force will often sign on with a contract company that provides additional reps for the pharmaceutical company. They may use the contract company reps as their exclusive sales force or may use the contract reps to supplement their own sales force. Contract sales forces are often used for the launch period of a new product when the manufacturer wants to get as much face-to-face time with physicians as possible.

From an employee point of view, the contract companies are a wonderful way to get into the business and learn the ropes. Entry requirements are usually less strict that the manufacturer's and they often offer flex-time positions.

The pros and cons of working for a contract company:

Contract companies offer fabulous benefits and great vacation schedules. No matter what contract you're on, your vacation accrual remains the same. If employed by a contract company, you may not do quite as much client entertaining in the evenings as you would if you were employed by the manufacturer. The average length of a contract is one year.

On the flip side, salaries can vary widely from contract to contract. One company may offer a low base salary and high commissions, and another may offer a higher base salary and lower commissions. You are also at the mercy of the contract: when the contract has expired, the pharmaceutical company may not renew it. If that is the case, the contract company may have another contract lined up with another company. If they don't, you will be looking for another job.

Contract company listing:

Dendrite International, Inc.
1405/1425 Route 206 South
Bedminster, NJ 07921
(908) 443-2000
http://www.drte.com

Innovex
Waterview Corporate Centre
Parsippany, NJ 07054 US
Phone: (888)-Innovex
(973) 257-4500
http://www.innovexglobal.com

Professional Detailing Inc.
Saddle River Executive Centre
1 Route 17 South
Saddle River, NJ 07458 US
Phone: (201) 818-8450
(800) 698-7491 (to apply)
http://www.pdi-inc.com

Pro-Pharma
24 Queen Street East, Suite 900
Brampton, Ontario L6V 1A3, Canada
(905) 459-9728
http://www.pro-pharma.com

Ventiv Health, Inc.
Vantage Court North
200 Cottontail Lane
Somerset, NJ 08873
(800) 416-0555
http://www.ventiv.com

Drug information:

The Physicians Desk Reference: Best bet is to find this book at your local library. Includes all prescribing information for all Rx drugs currently available in the US.

www.CoreyNahman.com Pharmaceutical news and information. Updated daily.

www.druginfonet.com Good Internet source for healthcare information including drug and disease information.

www.pharmacy.UMaryland.edu/UMDI/ World's first drug information service on the Internet. Submit questions to qualified pharmacy staff.

www.Rxlist.com Prescribing information for most drugs that are approved in the US.

Help with researching companies:

www.bloomberg.com Excellent resource for company financial data and news.

www.cato.com/biotech/bio-co.html List of all companies that produce pharmaceuticals and biologics.

www.hoovers.com Research companies and get useful company background and financial data for your interviews.

Pharmaceutical career websites:

www.biosnail.com

www.bioview.com

www.cafepharma.com A site with all things pharmaceutical.

www.careerbuilder.com

www.go2pharmsales.com

www.hirehealth.com Specialize in healthcare jobs including pharmaceutical.

www.hirerx.com

www.mannmedical.com Recruiters for the pharmaceutical, biotech, and medical device industry. I have used them myself and they are top notch.

www.medjobcity.com

www.medzilla.com Great site with lots of jobs for pharmaceutical and biotech professionals.

www.monster.com You have probably heard of this one. A multitude of jobs for all professions, including pharmaceutical.

www.pharmaceuticaljobsusa.com

www.pharmaceuticalsalesrecruiters.com

www.pharmajoblink.com

www.pharmareps.com

About pharmaceutical sales certification courses:

Many "certification" companies will tell you that you need to be "certified" to land a job as a pharmaceutical sales representative. This simply is not true. No pharmaceutical company, that I am aware of, will require that you have this "certification" to be hired with their company. Beware of certification companies who advertise on the big job boards. They advertise pharma sales job openings in all major cities at all times. My belief is that the jobs don't actually exist and that their goal is to get as many people as possible to send their resume so that they can "sell" them their certification program. Just for the record, they have had the exact same jobs listed in all those cities for over a year.

I do, however, recommend the live seminars offered by the American Pharmaceutical Sales Association (*www.apsaonline.org*) not because of the "certificate" that they offer but because of the quality of their live program. I have personally attended an ASPA seminar to audit it. They offer a truly interactive learning experience and participants can take a lot of what they have learned back to their interviews. The certificate alone won't land the job but if participants can learn something and apply it to interviews, now that makes a difference! The program offered by APSA is the only program that I recommend. Please don't confuse them with imitators who are charging a lot of money to get "certified" just for reading their book.

Professional résumé writers:

Marty Weitzman (NCRW, CPRW, JCTC) Has been writing résumés for professionals in the pharmaceutical industry for more than 25 years and comes with the best credentials in the business. Marty crafts the résumés himself and is particularly good at writing résumés for professionals who are transitioning to sales. Contact him at *www.pharmaceuticalsalesresumes.com* or at 1.800.967.3846.

CRI (www.careerresumes.com) Specialize in sales résumés. Each client is assigned two team members — a writer, who specializes in that client's function and industry, and an experienced job placement assistance professional whose background is in Human Resources. Contact person is Mark Bartz. His email address is *mark@careerresumes.com*.

Targeted Professional Résumé Distribution:

www.pharmaceuticalsalesinterviews.com (this is a service that I offer). I will send your résumé directly to over 150 pharmaceutical, medical, and biotech employers and recruiters' inbox.

TERRIFIC, TIMESAVING TEMPLATES:
Refer to these when preparing your correspondence

Informal thank you letter
(After the interview)

This letter should be handwritten on a small notecard to give it that personal touch. If you prefer to use a more formal approach, type it out on your personalized stationary. Send it immediately following your interview.

Your Name
Address
City, State, Zip
Phone

Date of interview

Ms. Manager Name
Title
Address
City, State, Zip

Dear Ms. Manager,

It was a pleasure meeting with you earlier today. I enjoyed learning more about ABC Pharmaceuticals.

I hope that I conveyed to you how excited I am about the prospect of working for you. My internships and part-time jobs in medical areas have given me a clear idea of what a pharmaceutical sales career would entail. I truly feel a calling for this type of work.

I know that you expect the search to last a few more weeks. In the meantime, please don't hesitate to call me if you need further information.

Many thanks for your consideration. I am looking forward to hearing from you!

Sincerely,
(Your name)

(*You may also want to add a sentence or two about something specific that was discussed during the interview in the second paragraph.)

Your Name

RESIGNATION LETTER

Address
Phone number
City, State, ZIP
Email address

Date

Name
Company
Street Address
City, State, Zip

Dear _____:

Please accept this letter as my formal resignation from my position with *(name of company)*. I have accepted a position as *(job title)* with *(name of company)* and my last date of employment will be *(date)*.

Although I have enjoyed working with you and my co-workers at *(name of employer)*, I feel I could not pass up this opportunity to take my career in a new and exciting direction.

In closing, I would like to express my deep gratitude to you for the training and guidance you have given me over the years. I will always be appreciative.

Sincerely,
(Your name)

Your Name

THANK YOU FOR THE REFERRAL

Address
Phone number
City, State, ZIP
Email address

Date

Name
Company
Street Address
City, State, Zip

Dear _____:

I want to thank you for your referral and for all of the help that you have given me during my job search. I am very grateful for your advice and support. If there is any way that I can help you in the future please let me know.

Again, thank you for all you have done for me.

Sincerely,
(Your name)

Your Name

LETTER OF ACCEPTANCE OF JOB OFFER

Address
Phone number
City, State, Zip
Email address

Date

Name
Company
Street Address
City, State, Zip

Dear _____:

This letter is my formal acceptance of your offer of employment with *(name of new employer)* as *(job title)*. I find all of the terms of employment you outlined in your letter acceptable, including the offer of a $_____ annual starting salary.

Today, I formally submitted my resignation with *(name of employer)*. My last date of employment will be *(date)*. If agreeable to you, I would like my first day of employment with *(new employer)* to begin on *(date)*, as I am eager to start my new position.

Thank you for the confidence you demonstrated by selecting me for this position and for the help you provided me with during the hiring process. I look forward to working with you.

Sincerely,
(Your name)

Your Name
LIST OF REFERENCES

Name
Phone number
Person's title
Company name
Address
City, State, Zip

Name
Phone number
Person's title
Company name
Address
City, State, Zip

Name
Phone number
Person's title
Company name
Address
City, State, Zip

Name
Phone number
Person's title
Company name
Address
City, State, Zip

Name
Phone number
Person's title
Company name
Address
City, State, Zip

Your Name
SALARY HISTORY

Company name
Address
City, State, Zip
Job Title:
Work dates: 00/00/00 to 00/00/00
Ending salary: $0.00

Company name
Address
City, State, Zip
Job Title:
Work dates: 00/00/00 to 00/00/00
Ending salary: $0.00

Company name
Address
City, State, Zip
Job Title:
Work dates: 00/00/00 to 00/00/00
Ending salary: $0.00

Company name
Address
City, State, Zip
Job Title:
Work dates: 00/00/00 to 00/00/00
Ending salary: $0.00

Make several copies of the **Lead Organizer** and the **Résumé Tracker** on the following pages to help you organize the information that you gather when you follow *3 Days to a Pharmaceutical Sales Job Interview.*

LEAD ORGANIZER:

Company name:
Division:

Contact person (Name, address, phone number, email address):

Date contacted:
How contacted: Additional leads from this contact:

Questions/Notes:

Which division has the opening?
What specialists do they call on?
Products?
Competing products?
Territory location?
Why is the position open?

Manager's name?
What looking for in an ideal candidate?
Hobbies/Interests?
Personality style?
Email address:
Home address:

RÉSUMÉ TRACKER:

Company name and address where résumé sent:

Person sent to:
Title:
Date sent:

Referring rep. name and number:
Thank you sent?

Gift sent? If so, what?

Interview date:
Follow up date:
Company history/information:

Notes: _____

"Real success is finding your lifework
in the work you love."
–*David McCullough*

**I wish you success, abundance,
and great self-fulfillment. Happy selling!**

About the author

Lisa Lane is the pharmaceutical sales industry's most visible author and consultant. Her pharmaceutical career began 18 years ago when she landed her first sales position right out of college. Since then, she has been an award-winning sales representative with Sandoz (Now Novartis), Glaxo Smith Kline and Schering Plough and has held positions as sales trainer and promotional planner.

Lisa is currently President of Drug Careers, Inc, a leading pharmaceutical sales career development company which provides curriculum for entry level training programs provided by the American Pharmaceutical Sales Association as well as for their University programs across the US. She is recognized as an authority in her field and is the recipient of a Marketing Destiny Award for creative sales programs. She has served as a career expert for many pharmaceutical career websites and the career sections of many newspapers and periodicals including "Career Builder", Sales and Marketing Magazine, The LA Times, The Baltimore Sun, The Miami Herald, The Chicago Tribune and over 20 others. She maintains daily contact with professionals in all areas of pharmaceutical sales, counsels her customers, and devotes a lot of time staying on top of current pharmaceutical news and information.

Give *3 Days To A Pharmaceutical Sales Job Interview* To Friends, Colleagues, And Loved Ones

CHECK YOUR LEADING BOOKSTORE
OR ORDER HERE

YES, I want _____ copies of *3 Days To A Pharmaceutical Sales Job Interview* at $29.95 each plus $4 shipping per book. Canadian orders must be accompanied by a postal money order in U.S. funds. Please allow two weeks for delivery.

☐ My check or money order for $_____ is enclosed.

☐ Please charge my credit card.   Type of card: _____

Name as it appears on credit card _____

Organization_____

Address _____

City/State/Zip_____

Phone_____ Email _____

Card # _____Expiration date _____

Signature_____

Please make your check payable and send it to:

Drug Careers Inc.
Box 543
Clarksburg, NJ 08510

Call your credit card order to: 800.247.6553

email: lisa@pharmaceuticalsalesinterviews.com

Index